Historical Problems:
Studies and Documents

Edited by
PROFESSOR G. R. ELTON
University of Cambridge

7
GOVERNMENT AND SOCIETY
IN FRANCE 1461-1661

In the same series

GOVERNMENT AND SOCIETY IN FRANCE 1461-1661

J. H. Shennan

University of Lancaster
Author of THE PARLEMENT OF PARIS

LONDON: GEORGE ALLEN AND UNWIN LTD
NEW YORK: BARNES AND NOBLE INC

FOR MARGARET

FIRST PUBLISHED IN 1969

SBN 04 901014 x *cloth*
SBN 04 901015 8 *paper*

PRINTED IN GREAT BRITAIN
in 10 *on* 11*pt Plantin type*
BY WILLMER BROTHERS LIMITED
BIRKENHEAD

GENERAL INTRODUCTION

The reader and the teacher of history might be forgiven for thinking that there are now too many series of historical documents in existence, all claiming to offer light on particular problems and all able to fulfil their claims. At any rate, the general editor of yet another series feels obliged to explain why he is helping one more collection of such volumes into existence.

One purpose of this series is to put at the disposal of the student original materials illustrating historical problems, but this is no longer anything out of the way. A little less usual is the decision to admit every sort of historical question: there are no barriers of time or place or theme. However, what really distinguishes this enterprise is the fact that it combines generous collections of documents with introductory essays long enough to explore the theme widely and deeply. In the doctrine of educationalists, it is the original documents that should be given to the student; in the experience of teachers, documents thrown naked before the untrained mind turn from pearls to paste. The study of history cannot be confined either to the learning up of results without a consideration of the foundations, or to a review of those foundations without the assistance of the expert mind. The task of teaching involves explanation and instruction, and these volumes recognize this possibly unfashionable fact. Beyond that, they enable the writers to say new and important things about their subject matter: to write history of an exploratory kind, which is the only important historical writing there is.

As a result, each volume will be a historical monograph worth the attention which all such monographs deserve, and each volume will stand on its own. While the format of the series is uniform, the contents will vary according to need. Some problems require the reconsideration which makes the known enlighteningly new; others need the attention of original research; yet others will have to enter controversy because the prevailing notions on many historical questions are demonstrably wrong. The authors of this series are free to treat their subject in whatever manner it seems to them to require. They will present some of their evidence for inspection and help the learner to see how history is written, but they will themselves also write history.

G.R.E.

AUTHOR'S NOTE

In order to span the considerable chronological and thematic range of this volume, it has been decided in some cases to add alphabetical subsections to the documents' numerical divisions. It is intended by this means to emphasize elements of continuity or of change within the context of particular themes.

CONTENTS

INTRODUCTION

Introduction

THE NATURE OF ROYAL AUTHORITY

Two distinguished historians of the *ancien régime*, commenting in 1955 upon the nature of the French state in the three centuries preceding the Revolution, have argued that a notion of absolutism existed from which the idea of despotism was excluded.[1] According to this notion, though the king's power was in the last resort unrestricted, it was customarily circumscribed by the tradition of French kingship, and any royal attempt at evading these inherited limitations would savour of arbitrariness (Doc. 1). This concept at once draws attention to those twin aspects of French history which together provide the necessary basis for an understanding of the period before 1789: the special nature of royal authority and the continuity of the monarchical tradition. The monarchy is the focussing lens through which French government and society should be viewed; it gave impetus to political action and point to social aspirations. This was true in Louis XIV's reign no less than in Louis XI's two hundred years before; indeed, it was scarcely less true in the days of Saint Louis some two centuries earlier still.

The abiding prestige of the French king, his ability to dominate the political scene, stemmed in the first place from his basic function, the obligation to provide justice for his subjects. Upon the royal seal of Hugh Capet, the first of the Capetians, the king was depicted as a judge, and that remained the essential role of his Valois and Bourbon successors. At their coronation each of them swore to govern justly and mercifully and the identification of the role of political sovereign with that of supreme judge inspired a legalistic concept of government which was as deeply felt in the seventeenth century as it had been in the fifteenth (Doc. 2). The king's right to administer the kingdom and to wield supreme executive power depended upon his prior right to dispense justice. He could and did empower his officials and counsellors not only to collect taxes, supervise the waging of wars and deal with a thousand and one administrative matters,

[1] F. Hartung and R. Mousnier, 'Quelques problèmes concernant la monarchie absolue', in *Rapport pour le Xe congrès international des sciences historiques*, Rome 1955, p. 12.

but also to judge on his behalf. It was even considered that problems of foreign policy had to be resolved by verdict of the royal judge.[2] Originally the king exercised his judicial authority in person or with the participation of his closest advisers. Joinville records how Saint Louis often chose to pass judgment informally, without either consultation or resort to the procedural trappings which already by the mid-thirteenth century were beginning to complicate the process of litigation.[3] In fact, one of the results of this formalization was the elimination of that sort of personal royal initiative. The king's justice was dispensed increasingly through the *curia regis*, and later, when that body could no longer cope with the volume and complexity of the law, through the *parlement* of Paris, itself an offshoot of the royal court. At the end of the fifteenth century no less perceptive an observer of the contemporary political scene than Nicolò Machiavelli paid tribute to the role of the *parlement* in maintaining for the French king the integrity of his kingdom.[4] The seventeenth-century French jurist, Loyseau, proclaimed a similar point of view when he wrote that France would have been a divided land, like Italy and Germany, had it not been for the *parlement*.[5] This institution more than any other could remind the king of his primary obligation to rule justly. For to rule justly implied respect for the law, and the laws of the kingdom and the countless civil and criminal judgments based upon these laws were enshrined in the *parlement*'s official records (Doc. 3). Briefly, in moments of political crisis, this doctrine became a subject for dispute as both sides—royal and *parlementaire*—or their supporters, pressed their case to untenable extremes (Doc. 4). However, the French like the English possessed no written constitution, and this lack of definition normally contributed to the maintenance of a generally accepted and less extravagant point of view (Doc. 5).

Of course all laws were not of equal weight; the legislation of one sovereign might subsequently be countermanded by another because it was no longer applicable, without provoking opposition, but some laws were considered immutable and any royal measures to dispense with them would certainly arouse serious objections. Included in this

[2] R. Mousnnier, 'L'évolution des institutions monarchiques en France et ses relations avec l'état social', in *Le dix-septième siècle*, vols LVII-LIX, 1963, p. 65.

[3] Jean, Sire de Joinville, *Histoire de Saint Louis*, pp. 184-5, in *Collection complète des mémoires relatifs à l'histoire de France depuis le règne de Philippe-Auguste jusqu'au commencement du dix-septième siècle*, ed. C. B. Petitot, Paris 1821-7.

[4] N. Machiavelli, *The Discourses of Niccolo Machiavelli*, ed. L. J. Walker, London 1950, i. 463.

[5] Cited in F. Lot and R. Fawtier, *Histoire des institutions Françaises au moyen âge*, Paris 1958, ii. 508.

category were the so-called fundamental laws, those primary rules upon which the state was built. The fundamental laws prescribed that government should be in the hands of a monarch who must be male, French, Catholic and legitimate, who must wield sovereign power within his kingdom, and who must not under any circumstances voluntarily alienate any part of his realm. These laws were not written down but they were sanctioned by custom, a sufficient guarantee since French law was itself chiefly based upon ancient local traditions.[6]

All these fundamental principles testified to the enormous prestige and authority which French kings traditionally enjoyed, but one of them served in a special way to reinforce that authority. This was the law of hereditary succession, according to which the sovereign derived his right to the throne from being the eldest relative in the direct male line of descent from the previous king. Whatever difficulties each new ruler might have to face, the legality of his position gave him an immediate and overwhelming advantage (Doc. 6). From Hugh Capet's accession in 987 to Louis XVI's death on the scaffold in 1794 no French king was deposed or executed, nor did any succeed to the throne in defiance of that law. This fact, perhaps not generally appreciated, does much to explain the monarchy's permanent and unshakeable hold upon affairs.

There was another kind of law to which the king was expected to adhere, the commandments of God, which set standards of Christian justice and morality which it was his duty to enforce. The quasi-spiritual role of the monarchy may be traced back beyond the Capetian line: Charlemagne's son, Louis the Pious, was anointed at his crowning with sacred oils. Henceforth the coronation became a religious ceremony, investing each successive ruler with unique authority. From these Carolingian origins the Capetians, Valois and Bourbons inherited the peculiar prestige attached to the coronation. The king became God's lieutenant on earth, *le roi très chrétien,* whose task it was to establish in his kingdom a régime which would reflect divine justice, however imperfectly. With this close relationship between the spiritual and temporal roles of the Crown went another royal attribute, the claim to exercise miraculous powers. Hugh Capet's son, Robert the Pious, was thought by his contemporaries to possess the gift of curing all ailments. The power was believed to be transmitted by heredity though from the reign of Robert's grandson, Philip I, it was considered to apply only to the very widespread disease of scrofula. Until the eighteenth century the thaumaturgic gift was accepted without question as one of the marks of legitimate French

[6] A. Lemaire, *Les lois fondamentales de la monarchie Française,* Paris 1907, *passim.*

kingship.[7] The religious framework in which the monarchy func-
tioned had the effect—as did the king's judicial role with which it
was intimately linked—of curbing the exercise of royal power, yet
at the same time adding enormously to its weight and influence
(Doc. 7).

The subject of the crown's relationship with the Catholic church
must be examined in further detail. The quarrel between Philip the
Fair and Pope Boniface VIII over the king's right to tax the French
clergy was part of a broader dispute about the respective roles of king
and pope in the French church, out of which emerged the principles
of Gallicanism. The early Capetians had interfered regularly in the
appointment of prelates, nominating them personally or even selling
the right of nomination to their friends, thus flouting the principle
of self-governing election by ecclesiastical chapters which had previously prevailed in all major benefices. The eleventh-century investi-
ture contest shifted the balance once more in favour of the earlier
system, though the king kept the right to draw revenue from vacant
benefices—the so-called secular *régale*—and his approval was required both before election was made and before the successful candidate was consecrated. Thus he kept a firm control over the French
church, a control which seemed in no way improper since his coronation had already made him a quasi-spiritual figure, the secular arm of
the Christian Church in France. The king wielded an undisputed right
to summon and preside over assemblies of his prelates in order to
debate matters affecting the French Church, and he swore at his
coronation to preserve the canonical privileges, rights and immunities, including those of self-government, which had become traditional in the French church. The significance of this close bond
between king and church became clear when the papacy sought to
extend its influence in the French kingdom. Hence the quarrel between Philip and Boniface and the long battle which followed over
the succeeding century and a half, culminating in the publication of
the celebrated edict of 1438, the Pragmatic Sanction of Bourges.

This law confirmed the ancient tradition in support of the principle of election to major benefices in France, and it also indirectly
confirmed the king's intimate involvement in the procedure, and his
right to nominate candidates to the electors. Where minor benefices
were concerned, the rights of those customarily exercising them were
safeguarded, and in both spheres the possibilities of papal intervention were strictly limited. The pope's claim to exact money from the
holders of benefices in France in the form of annates, was also denied
and in this matter, too, the edict offered a re-statement of a long held

[7] M. Bloch, *Les rois thaumaturges*, Paris 1924, *passim*.

Gallican position. The Pragmatic Sanction represented the quint-essential statement of Gallicanism: it reiterated principles that were embodied in the jurisprudence of the country's law courts and were in complete accord with the customs of the kingdom. It had been drawn up after solemn deliberation with royal advisers, princes, nobles, prelates and lawyers, and published and registered by the *parlement* of Paris. Charles VII acknowledged it as a law to be observed 'inviolably and for ever'.[8]

Such protestations, however, bound neither Charles himself nor his successors, and in 1461 his son, Louis XI, abrogated the Pragmatic Sanction in favour of closer relations with the papacy. In 1472 he signed a concordat with the pope, Sixtus IV, whereby the pope was to appoint to all major benefices upon the king's recommendation and the papal annates were to be restored. This agreement was challenged after the king's death by French lawyers and by the Estates-General and the precise relationship between Paris and Rome remained obscure throughout the reigns of Charles VIII and Louis XII. Then in 1516, Francis I concluded the Concordat of Bologna with Pope Leo X, an agreement which removed the equivocations of his predecessors' position by clearly abolishing the old system of electoral self-government for bishoprics, abbeys and priories, substituting the principle of royal nomination and papal appointment and preparing the way for the re-establishment of the payment of papal annates (Doc. 8).

The question must be asked why both Louis XI and Francis I should be willing to make an arrangement with the papacy which involved the recognition of the latter's right to intervene—in however limited a fashion—in the appointment of French prelates and also to extract certain revenues from them. The answer is not to be found, paradoxically, in any weakness on the French side but rather in the crown's increasing awareness of its own importance. During the fifteenth century the monarchy had led the victorious struggle to dislodge the English from their possessions in France and in so doing it had acquired a massive prestige in the country which enabled it to ask for and to receive unprecedented financial assistance with which to support the beginnings of a regular royal army. The authority of the Papacy, on the other hand, had not recovered from the Great Schism and a succession of Renaissance popes did nothing to restore Christian morale. The time seemed ripe for the king to assert his authority in that one sphere—the religious—in which he might still be expected to retain an inferiority complex. After the Concordat of 1516 Francis I controlled some hundred archbishoprics and bishoprics and about five hundred abbeys. The king's nomination would in

---

[8] V. Martin, *Les origines du Gallicanisme*, 2 vols, Paris 1939, provides the most detailed analysis of this affair.

B

future be much more important than the Pope's confirmation, though the latter was by no means discounted (Doc. 9). At a time when the king was beginning to extract revenue from assemblies of bishops and abbots in the form of 'free gifts', his power of appointment to senior positions in the church was an especially useful one. In financial terms, therefore, the payment of annates was a small price to pay for the large rewards which the crown could hope to extract from a largely subservient clergy; in political terms the papacy had to be content with a largely honorific though honourable role, for it had never been a tenet of Gallican doctrine to sever France's link with Rome. Only occasionally in the future would the Papacy be able to exert a direct influence over French affairs (Docs. 10 and 11).

Though it appears that the French crown was tightening its hold over the French church and that its intention was to do precisely that, it is also indisputable that the crown had a great deal of authority over the church even before the Concordats of 1472 and 1516. It is arguable that the terms of the Pragmatic Sanction itself ensured that only those candidates who met with royal approval could expect to be successful. There seems therefore to be a danger of exaggerating the significance of the Concordats, especially that of 1516. Yet at the time, clerics and lawyers combined in intense opposition to Francis I's measure. The *parlement* of Paris condemned it as being contrary to the honour of God, the liberties of the church, the honour of the king and the well-being of his kingdom, and certainly the king's action in depriving the church of ancient privileges, which it was considered his duty to defend, was widely held to be arbitrary and therefore of dubious validity.[9] In fact, the Pragmatic Sanction continued to find more favour among jurists and clergy than the Concordat until the end of the *ancien régime,* and a succession of Assemblies of Clergy tirelessly demanded its reimposition. The strength and persistence of the opposition does suggest that the agreement reached in 1516 between the French king and Pope Leo X did indeed represent a novel and drastic step. In fact, the two points of view are not incompatible. In legal and theoretical terms, not terms lightly to be dismissed in an age which depended so heavily upon moral persuasion, the Concordat represented a flagrantly unjust act; in practical terms it made little difference. Because it made little difference, Francis I and his Valois and Bourbon successors were all able to enforce it, in spite of the weight of opinion against it. Of course, the crown enjoyed great prestige and authority during the reign of Francis I; in the eighteenth century, when that was not the case, the comparable dispute over the implementation of the papal bull *Unigenitus* brought the crown to

[9] R. Doucet, *Etude sur le gouvernement de François Ier dans ses rapports avec le parlement de Paris,* Paris 1921, i. 104.

the edge of disaster. The change of procedure introduced by the Concordat did not stimulate the nomination of more suitable aspirants for high ecclesiastical office, although the cabals and manoeuvres preceding an election, the rival pressures exerted by important local families, had also inevitably produced a number of unsatisfactory results (Docs. 15 and 18b). The king was responsible for some unfortunate appointments, particularly in the sixteenth century, when some of his episcopal nominees even defected to the protestant camp! But under Henry IV and Louis XIII royal appointments were for the most part scrupulously made, and few criticisms could be levelled against their candidates' suitability for high office.[10]

The Concordat of Bologna reinforced the king's authority over the church and gave it a great psychological boost at a vital moment, when Lutheranism was about to take hold in the Holy Roman Empire. Circumstances forced Luther to accept the state as the necessary protector of the spiritual order, and since in France the secular ruler already occupied a dominant position in ecclesiastical matters there was no political reason for the French crown to embrace the new faith. Even if there had been it is most unlikely that *le roi très chrétien,* whose inherited prestige depended so much upon the preservation of religious orthodoxy, would have been willing to risk a change. In fact, though Francis I was a shrewd enough politician to ally with Lutheranism abroad in order to embarrass his chief adversary, the Emperor Charles V, and though at home he tended to distinguish between out-and-out reformers and humanists like Lefèvre d'Etaples with whom he rather sympathized, by the later years of his reign he was an unequivocal and ruthless enemy of German protestantism. Through the agency of the *parlement* of Paris, Lutheran works were censored, printers were required to work on approved premises, booksellers forbidden to sell unauthorized volumes and severe punishments were meted out against those who were convicted.[11]

Therefore Lutheranism made little headway in France; the real threat came from Calvinism which, far from depending upon the support of the secular power, was capable of organizing itself as a revolutionary movement against the government. The Wars of Religion followed, and though the government's attitude varied between one of harsh intolerance and unwilling moderation there was no possibility of any basic change in the attitude of the monarchy until an unpredictable series of events brought the Huguenot Henry of Navarre

[10] F. Olivier-Martin, *Histoire du droit Français des origines à la Révolution,* Paris 1948, p. 476.
[11] E. Maugis, *Histoire du parlement de Paris de l'avènement des rois Valois à la mort d'Henri IV,* 3 vols, Paris 1913–16, ii. 310 et seq.

to the French throne. His decision to change his faith once more and return to the orthodox fold was more than a shrewd or cynical political manoeuvre; it was a recognition of the fundamental nature of the crown's catholicity (Doc. 11). This catholicity, though, remained Gallican, and in a variety of areas not previously mentioned in this essay, but all forming part of the ancient Gallican tradition—the pope's authority *vis-à-vis* that of an oecumenical council, the rights of the French bishops *vis-à-vis* dogmatic papal pronouncements—the crown and the papacy continued their disputes over authority until the end of the *ancien régime*. But the French monarchy weathered the Reformation storm, though not without enduring a period of grave crisis, and emerged virtually unaffected, its authority still firmly based upon principles which Henry IV and his predecessors had considered it vital to preserve. During the seventeenth century the problem of the Huguenots steadily diminished, and those religious issues which did cause trouble for the government, Gallicanism and later Jansenism, occurred within the framework of traditional orthodoxy (Doc. 12).

Another limitation upon the exercise of royal authority was the tradition that the king should seek advice before taking important decisions on any of the wide-ranging and multitudinous affairs for which he was responsible (Doc. 13). This idea too was of very long standing, stemming originally from the strong Germanic tradition of judgment by peers and subsequently translated into feudal terms under which a vassal was obliged to proffer advice to his lord if required to do so. For a long time his counsellors were the great barons who frequented the royal court, many of whom were honoured by the king with domestic titles like butler, chamberlain or constable, and the country's leading prelates. They dominated the *curia regis* until the twelfth century when government was beginning to require a degree of sophistication and expertise which they were not able to provide. Not that their advisory role ceased. That was by no means the case, though the manner in which it was exercised did change. The king came to rely increasingly for advice upon a small body of advisers, dominated by professional paid counsellors, usually legists, who could provide expert opinions on judicial, financial and administrative matters. Out of this inner council the *parlement* eventually emerged. Out of the great baronial gatherings at which all important decisions had once been taken emerged the Estates-General. These institutions sought to maintain, with varying success, the advisory role with which they had been associated from the beginning. However, they were not the exclusive channels through which the sovereign could receive guidance. The royal council itself survived the loss of various other components which in the course of time acquired an independent existence—not only the *parlement* and the Estates-General, but also, for example, the *chambre des comptes* and the *grand conseil*, established respectively in 1320 and 1497—and continued to provide an important source of advice for the sovereign. Its shape and its membership continued to fluctuate until the end of the *ancien régime*. Especially in the first half of the sixteenth century its structure and organization were so fluid as to be almost indefinable, save at particular moments for particular purposes. Later in the century, in the reigns of Henry III and Henry IV, the situation is rather less obscure, as various specialized sub-divisions of the council became vaguely discernible. Later still, under Louis XIII, the council was well enough organized, on occasion, to carry out its own advice, even before the king was informed (Doc. 14).

Equally variable was its membership. Louis XI promised to recruit six *bourgeois*, six members of the *parlement*, and six members of the University of Paris to his council. Under Francis I and Henry II the princes and peers, and the great officers of the crown, the constable, admiral, *grand'maître* and chancellor, gave the council an aristocratic appearance that masked the influence of more humbly born experts. During the religious wars the great nobility did in fact reassert its dominance, though at the same time the new offices of the secretaries of state in the royal council, held by men of recent middle-class or lesser noble origins and destined to play a significant role in the future, were being established.[12] It is worth noting that there was nothing unique about Louis XIV's much-publicized decision to employ men of humble origin as councillors. The process tended to be cyclical: the replacement as royal advisors of such men as the great Condé by the Colberts and the Phélypeaux may be compared with earlier substitutions—the appearance of influential secretaries of state like Villeroy, to counter the warring factions of Guise and Montmorency, which after Henry II's death troubled the council chamber and threatened the existence of the state itself; or the appearance of new men learned in the law, the *magistri*, who earlier still had ousted the great barons and prelates from the *curia regis*.

Therefore, although the fundamental law required the king to be sovereign, so that no other institution or individual should challenge his ultimate authority in the state, there were a good many markers to indicate the true path along which he ought to tread. Nor was this a purely negative concept, intended only to restrict the crown's freedom of action. It had a very positive side too, for the state was made up of a variety of organizations and groups, each possessing rights of its own, rights moreover that were legally guaranteed, forming part of the inherited body of law which the king was bound to respect.

[12] R. Doucet, *Les institutions de la France aue XVI siècle*, Paris 1948, i. 131-40.

Our own experience of modern highly centralized states may easily cause us to misunderstand the nature of the French state in the fifteenth, sixteenth and seventeenth centuries. It was a federation, given unity and coherence by the crown, but composed of distinct, if sometimes overlapping groups, whose members saw no reason to cede their rights and privileges and thus lose their separate identity.

THE FIRST ESTATE

The clergy formed the first estate of the realm, though from the middle of the fifteenth century its pre-eminence was being undermined in a number of areas. Certainly in political affairs its influence was diminishing, and the crown came to rely increasingly upon lay advisers, whose reward for service was sometimes unwillingly provided by the church (Doc. 15). Nevertheless, the church's prestige remained enormous and all-pervading: the king's authority was closely linked with that of the church through his coronation, and the principles by which he was expected to govern were Christian principles.

Socially there was a wide gulf between the extremes of the ecclesiastical spectrum. The clergy may be divided into two groups, secular and regular, the former being those clerics who were not members of religious communities and the latter those who were. Until the middle of the sixteenth century, all religious orders in France were bound by the rule of St Augustine, St Benedict, or St Francis; after that date, the Society of Jesus provided a fourth alternative. They were governed either through a hierarchy of abbots and priors, or by a general (usually resident at Rome) and his provincial representatives. At the head of the secular clergy were the archbishops and bishops. Usually, though not invariably, these were noblemen—some were even peers —whilst at the other extreme most village priests were scarcely distinguishable in their mode of life from their humble parishioners. In between came the members of cathedral chapters appointed to assist the bishops in the administration of their diocese. Some of these chapters tended to be the preserve of the nobility—the king himself was the first of the *chanoines-comtes de Lyon*; others had no such social limitations. All the members of the first estate however, noble and non-noble, prelate and *curé*, shared the prestige which attached to their spiritual calling. In the countryside the priest was often the only man in his parish who could read and write; yet it was not his relative erudition but his unique role as a means to salvation which impressed a deeply religious society. Equally the archbishops and bishops, beneath their mundane magnificence and away from their great Gothic cathedrals, remained the awesome prophets of that other world which everyone knew to be both imminent and eternal (Doc. 16).

But the first estate was not unified by prestige alone; it possessed a number of other tangible privileges. Its members had certain tax concessions.[13] The question of the king's right to tax the clergy in France had precipitated the famous quarrel between Philip the Fair and Pope Boniface VIII at the end of the thirteenth century. In the fifteenth century the king changed his tactics. He no longer tried to raise grants from the clergy by dealing directly with the Papacy; instead he summoned assemblies of bishops and abbots to obtain revenue, not in the form of taxation but as a free gift, the implication being that such gifts were exceptional and not an obligation. This state of affairs was regulated by the contract of Poissy in 1561. According to this contract the clergy agreed to pay the king an annual sum of 1,600,000 *livres* for six years and to make a further less onerous grant over the following ten years (Doc. 17). In 1577 the clergy was forced to continue its subsidies, the new agreement involving an annual grant of 1,300,000 *livres* for ten years. This sum became a permanent annual payment intended to meet the interest debt owed to government investors, and in addition the clergy voted a *don gratuit* every five years, a sum which grew gradually larger, reaching the highest totals in times of war. Although it is dangerous to generalize about a theme on which the evidence is scanty, there seems little doubt that overall the clergy's contributions represented a considerable measure of financial privilege.

Besides, the clergy received additional safeguards for making concessions in the first place. Their financial offerings were to be freely voted at General Assemblies held every five years. These meetings were composed of deputies elected from the various ecclesiastical provinces of the kingdom. Not all French clerics were represented, for those in certain provinces incorporated into the kingdom after the contract of Poissy chose to make their own bargain with the crown. The clergy of Hainault were such a group. The deputies appointed by those who were concerned usually met in Paris. There they were informed of the amount which the king was seeking, and then negotiations began with his agents. When a figure was agreed, contracts were signed by representatives of both sides so that the donation was on a strictly legal basis and limited to a specific period of time. In this way too the idea that the clergy was not obliged to make financial contributions to the state was preserved. Indeed, although such contributions were always made, there was no question of the crown automatically getting what it demanded. In 1641, for example, Richelieu had to be satisfied with half a million *livres* less than he wanted.[14]

[13] Doucet, *Les institutions de la France*, ii. 831.
[14] M. Marion, *Dictionnaire des institutions de la France aux XVIIᵉ et XVIIIᵉ siècles*, Paris 1923, p.105.

In order to safeguard the clergy's interests and privileges in the years when the Assembly was not in session, two general agents were elected at each quinquennial session to serve for the following five years (Doc. 18).

The traditional means employed by the crown to raise revenue from the clergy was by resort to the *décime*, or tenth. Usually the tenth was first approved by an assembly of the clergy at any level from that of the General Assembly down to the diocesan, though almost invariably this prior consent was a formality. In 1561, in the Contract of Poissy, the system of tenths was regulated. Henceforth, each General Assembly and the two agents appointed by it were responsible for raising the tenths. A financial organization was gradually evolved, almost totally independent of the royal exchequer, to assess and collect the money and arbitrate any disputes. The tenth was a direct tax, exacting in theory from each benefice-holder a sum equal to one-tenth of his revenue. In practice the amount was probably less, and in the collecting a number of serious inequalities emerged between regions. From 1636 cardinals received virtual exemption from the tenth, though ten years later the contribution was extended to include the Society of Jesus in France. On the whole, the system was tolerably efficient and effective. Certainly, loans on the tenth which the first estate was forced to incur in order to provide the king with immediate lump sums were readily available because its credit was good, rather better in fact than that of the crown.

The privilege of an autonomous taxation system exempted the clergy from a number of onerous taxes (Doc. 10). They did not have to contribute to the *taille personnelle*, the *aides* or the *gabelle* or salt tax, and they were also free from the *corvée*, the obligation to provide public labour for a number of days each year. They were not obliged either to provide accommodation for the king's soldiers or to contribute to the upkeep of roads and bridges. Finally, their independent financial system was matched by an independent judicial organization.

The church's judicial authority was exercised in the main by the *official*, who was generally appointed by the bishop to act on the diocesan level. However the church courts, or *officialités*, were graded to conform with the various steps in the ecclesiastical hierarchy, archidiaconal, episcopal, archiepiscopal and primatial, and there was a system of appeal from the lower tribunal to its immediate superior. Originally the jurisdiction of these courts had been very wide, but from the fourteenth century the royal courts began to challenge their authority and by the close of the fifteenth century the jurisdictional battle had been settled in favour of the secular power. By the mid-seventeenth century only purely spiritual issues, referring for example to the administration of the sacraments, remained totally within the

competence of the *officialités* (Doc. 20). Nevertheless, the two jurisdictions continued to co-exist. Indeed, as long as society retained its
deeply religious sense, the *officialité*, a visible sign of the church's
authority, would not lose its prestige.[15]

THE SECOND ESTATE

The nobility constituted the second estate of the realm. Because noble
status was held by men and women of widely differing condition a
single group classification might seem valueless. That is not the case,
however, for the possession of nobility provided the holder, whether
he was a prince of the royal blood living in Paris or Versailles, or a
humble *hobereau* from the Auvergne, with certain privileges which
all noblemen shared; the fact that different classes of noblemen might
have little else in common was less important. These privileges bestowed real advantages as well as great social prestige. Chief amongst
the former was exemption from the *taille personnelle*, the most onerous
of royal taxes. Nobility also brought exemption from the *corvée*
and the *gabelle*. Nor was a nobleman required to serve in the militia
or to quarter royal troops. In the judicial sphere he was entitled to
have cases in which he was involved tried in the first instance at no
less than bailiwick level, that is by the tribunal immediately below the
sovereign court. He also enjoyed certain honorific rights in any public
gathering, large or small, at which he was present (Doc. 21). However, all the privileges of noble status added together mattered less
to the nobleman than the *fact* of his nobility. It was this awareness of
his exclusive position which gave coherence to the second estate and
an aura of stability and permanence to the political order. Such an
aura remained acceptable for so long because of the enduring prestige
of the monarch, himself the greatest nobleman in the land, and because the noble class was not a closed caste inaccessible to ambitious
men.[16]

Noble status was variously acquired. It might be the fortuitous
accident of birth: a father—though not a mother—who already possessed hereditary nobility passed on that attribute to his sons and
daughters. It generally took three generations of personal nobility to
acquire an hereditary title and access to the *noblesse de race* (Doc. 22).
Within that classification there were of course degrees of prestige
between, for example, the grandson of a magistrate who had acquired

[15] Olivier-Martin, *Histoire du droit Français*, pp. 383-6; Marion, *Dictionnaire*,
pp. 107, 407.
[16] G. Zeller, *Les institutions de la France au XVIe siècle*, Paris 1948, pp. 12-15;
F. L. Ford, *Robe and Sword*, Cambridge, Mass. 1962 edition, pp. 27-9.

personal noble status through his membership of a sovereign court and a representative of one of the dwindling number of ancient families, like the Montmorency or the La Rochefoucauld. The chief representatives of the *noblesse de race* were to be found at court. First came the *enfants de France*, the children and grandchildren of the reigning monarch and sometimes the nephews as well, and then the princes and princesses of the royal blood, collateral relatives of the sovereign. Next came the peers. Originally, in the second half of the twelfth century, the title evidently referred to a group of the king's most powerful vassals who demanded the right to assist at any judgment in which one of their own number was involved. This tradition was maintained by their successors' right to a place in the *parlement* of Paris. At first their number was restricted to twelve, six layman and six clerics, the Dukes of Normandy, Burgundy and Acquitaine, and the Counts of Flanders, Toulouse and Champagne, the Archbishop of Rheims and the Bishops of Laon, Langres, Beauvais, Châlons-sur-Marne and Noyon (Doc. 16a). After 1600, however, the number of lay peerages multiplied. After the peers came the dukes, then the marquises and counts.[17]

Noblesse de race, therefore, covered a broad social spectrum; it represented less a means of acquiring noble status than the final and permanent acknowledgement of that status. There were a number of means by which this enviable state could be achieved besides the accident of birth (Doc. 23). One was through the acquisition of certain offices. Some of these offices, like that of chancellor or keeper of the seals, imparted complete nobility to the holder; others, like that of counsellor in the *parlement*, gave only personal nobility, and at least until 1644, that, together with the expectation of an hereditary title for the grandson who exercised the same or a similar honourable office as that of his father and grandfather, had to suffice (Doc. 24). It was also possible to reach the *noblesse de race* through military service, though here too the personal honour came first and hereditary noble status only in the third generation. The most frequent channel, however, gradually became that of straightforward purchase, and French kings, who were constantly in need of additional resources, showed themselves increasingly ready to bestow nobility in return for hard cash. Sometimes nobility thus acquired was only for the purchaser himself, but if sufficient money was forthcoming it was usually possible to buy hereditary nobility at once (Doc. 25). Thus nobility, however acquired, was either hereditary—*noblesse de race*—or per-

[17] H. Brocher, *Le rang et l'etiquette sous l'ancien régime*, pp. 1-20.

sonal.[18] If the latter, it was frequently though not invariably converted into the former in succeeding generations. Frequent attempts were also made to usurp noble status, and neither the complaints of the nobility nor the strictures of the crown seemed very effective deterrents. Proof of nobility depended either on direct documentary evidence or on indirect documentary evidence joined to a long and undisputed tradition; ultimately every individual's claim depended upon the crown's acceptance of his judicial case (Doc. 26).

As with the crown, noble status involved responsibility as well as privilege, obligations as well as rights. The nobleman's prime obligation, of course, was to serve the king as a soldier; for that reason he was dispensed from the fiscal burdens which were originally a substitute for military service. By the reign of Louis XI a permanent mercenary force existed but the traditional feudal role of the nobility survived through the mechanism of the *ban et arrière-ban*. All noblemen—or rather all holders of fiefs, a definition which included a number of non-nobles—were expected to serve for forty days every year, a period increased to three months if it did not include service abroad. Those who could not attend in person were expected to depute a substitute or pay taxes instead (Doc. 27). The feudal host was still being summoned in Louis XIII's reign, though that king was extremely scathing about the behaviour of his noble retainers who were apparently unable to endure more than a day or two of active service before withdrawing to their estates.[19]

The nobleman was obliged to hold himself in readiness for royal service in any capacity, not necessarily a military one only, and he had besides a number of more general obligations like that of providing material and moral support for his entourage and his dependants. Such moral obligations were difficult to enforce at law though they did constitute aspects of *la vie exemplaire*, the standard of behaviour to which all noblemen were expected to conform. However, there were certain offences against this standard which were susceptible of legal redress, involving the penalty of forfeiture of nobility. A criminal conviction, for example, would certainly result in deprivation of noble status. But it was not only criminal conduct which carried that penalty. In the fourteenth century the juridical idea of *dérogeance* appeared, extending the application of forfeiture to new spheres which varied

---

[18] As with so many other aspects of this period, regulations governing noble status turn out to be contradictory and inconsistent. One persistent belief was that more than four generations of nobility were required for the attainment of the supreme honours of the second estate, yet the king was frequently disposed to ignore it (Doc. 25d). In fact, the division between personal and hereditary nobility is the only consistently valid distinction that can be made.

[19] Marion, *Dictionnare*, p. 34; Lot and Fawtier, *Histoire des institutions Françaises*, ii, 531-2.

according to the peculiarities of local customary law. In Normandy, for example, a man forfeited his nobility if he no longer had the means to support his rank. Forfeiture was the penalty all over France for those noblemen who indulged in trade or commercial ventures (though glass-making was a notable exception), who performed manual labour, other than on their own land, or who held certain professional appointments, like that of solicitor, which were not considered compatible with noble status. Deprivation thus incurred was not necessarily permanent in every part of the country; in Brittany and in Artois it was possible to regain nobility automatically once the cause of *dérogeance* had been removed (Doc. 28). The principle of *la vie exemplaire* helped to preserve a sense of social equilibrium in the state. Noblemen, like everybody else, were limited by their obligations; profitable commercial activities were the privilege of those who paid taxes.[20]

THE THIRD ESTATE

Finally, after the king, clergy and nobility came the third estate. Once more a single category covers a wide variety of men and conditions, from wealthy representatives of the *bourgeois* class, to the Burgundian serf. The *bourgeois* were privileged members of a community, possessing clearly defined rights and obligations. This status might be acquired by birth or by a period of residence within a town: in Paris that period was one year and one day. In return for this honour, the *bourgeois* paid a small tax, often in kind, at least during the sixteenth century, and a number of other exceptional payments besides. In addition he was expected to form part of the town militia to keep watch during the hours of darkness, though this duty was often commuted into a money payment. The privileges of the *bourgeois* amply compensated however for these obligations. In particular he was excused payment of the *taille*. He enjoyed numerous other economic and legal advantages, including fishing and hunting rights. He also took a part in administering his community, in organizing the collection of municipal taxes and in exercising certain judicial rights within the community. Like a nobleman he was permitted to carry arms; within the town he was a figure of influence and prestige (Doc. 29).[21]

The great mass of the third estate however was made up of *roturiers*, free men living either in towns or in the countryside. In origin they all came from the servile class, and though all had acquired their freedom their rights and obligations in judicial terms

[20] Olivier-Martin, *Histoire du droit Français*, pp. 639-42.
[21] J. Ellul, *Histoire des institutions de l'époque Franque à la révolution*, Paris 1962, pp. 200-202, 287-90.

were not all the same, for the charters, individual and collective which
guaranteed that freedom revealed considerable variations (Doc. 30).
In some parts of the country ancient feudal dues like the *taille seig-
neuriale* persisted; in Brittany, even the seigneur's right to demand
accommodation from his vassals survived well into the sixteenth
century.[22]

At the very bottom of the social scale came the serf. Most of the
onerous personal obligations which afflicted the servile population in
the middle ages had been removed. They survived in a few small
areas, though for the most part in an attenuated form and were increasingly looked upon as anachronistic (Doc. 31).

THE POLITICAL ORGANIZATION OF THE ESTATES

Although the juridical division of king, clergy, nobility and third
estate provides a necessary, permanent framework against which to
interpret changing patterns, it does not contribute to an understanding of how the various elements co-operated in government, and it
suggests a misleading social rigidity. In fact the areas of common
ground, the links uniting the crown and the estates, and the strong
element of social mobility offer the best hope of understanding the
complexities of the French state during this period. The most important political organization to unite all the elements in the state was
the Estates-General. This institution grew out of the seminal conflict
between Philip the Fair and Boniface VIII though it also reflected
the traditional belief in the need to offer counsel to the sovereign. Its
membership provides an immediate insight into the shifting pattern
of French government and society. It was the king's prerogative to
summon whomever he pleased to counsel him and in the first part of
the fourteenth century he invited individual prelates and barons. Behind the form of invitation lay the feudal idea of the vassal's obligation to his lord. The lay and ecclesiastical vassals were summoned as
lords of the various *seigneuries* into which France, outside the boundaries of the royal domain, was divided. The *seigneurie* was both an
area of land and of jurisdiction, attached to the king's realm by feudal
ties and by the crown's particular prestige. With the growth in royal
authority the judicial power of the *seigneur* was undermined by the
king's judges. Although the seignorial courts remained competent
to deal with a number of cases until the end of the *ancien régime,* by
the seventeenth century they were being closely supervised by royal
officials and long before then the use of the appeal and of the legal
doctrines of *cas royaux* and *prévention* had underlined the pre-

[22] Doucet, *Les institutions de la France,* ii. 491.

eminence of the king's justice (Doc. 13).[23] Similarly, the possession of land which had once implied a feudal contract with mutual obligations between king and vassal, and, if the vassal chose to sub-lease part of his domain, between vassal and tenant, became an independent patrimonial right. Kings began to create *seigneuries* and distribute them, sometimes selling them to men of non-noble status who thus acquired some of the prestige of noble rank and some of the obligations too, like service in the feudal levy (Doc. 27). As the situation changed in the course of the fourteenth and fifteenth centuries the king ceased to summon his prelates and barons as individual holders of fiefs. Instead he called them by estate, clerical and noble.

He also invited representatives of the towns. Here too changes were taking place. To begin with, the towns had undermined the static feudal order where land, not money, was of fundamental importance. The life of a new town began with a royal or seignorial charter which bestowed widely differing rights and obligations upon the members of each new community. All the towns however fell into one of two broad categories—they were either part of the surrounding *seigneurie* or they themselves became *seigneuries*. Both categories represented a new source of wealth and power which survived the feudal context in which they first appeared. They possessed a certain financial autonomy: the right to assess and collect taxes for the upkeep and defence of the municipality and to administer their own accounts provided the town officials with their chief responsibility. A great many towns also possessed judicial powers, civil and criminal in the first instance, although there was little uniformity about the manner in which their authority was exercised. Judicial power might be vested in the mayor, in a nominee of the aldermen, in a jury of the town's *bourgeois* or in a commission elected from amongst the aldermen. Closely associated with judicial authority was the exercise of police powers by which was understood the regulation and supervision of town life in general, its hospitals and prisons, its food supplies, its roads and buildings, its commercial activities and its military security (Doc. 32). Education, sometimes to university level as at Bourges, was likewise in the hands of the municipal authorities.[24]

But there was another element of change affecting the urban scene: the increasing intervention of the king. This intervention was not

[23] The *cas royaux* were those cases, including the debasement of the royal coinage, highway robbery and all matters appertaining to ennoblement or legitimization, which involved the king's person or his rights and were brought before the royal courts in the first instance. *Prévention* was a legal theory in favour of the king's right to intervene in the sphere of seignorial justice in any cases of dilatoriness.

[24] Doucet, *Les institutions de la France*, i. 381.

always detrimental to the town and it would be a mistake to assume that the traditional independence of the towns was over before the seventeenth century. It is true that long before then French kings were intervening often in a very arbitrary fashion to amend or annul existing town charters. On the other hand one of the worst offenders in this regard, Louis XI, also extended municipal privileges to a number of towns which had not held them previously.[25] Of course his intention was less to limit his own authority than to demonstrate that it was the source of all such privileged régimes. His successors took the opportunity afforded by each renewal of a town charter to modify the existing constitution in favour of greater royal control. In particular the crown was concerned with municipal autonomy in financial matters. By the mid-fifteenth century the towns were universally dominated by the rich *bourgeois* class whose control over urban resources the king was anxious to break. In 1515 Francis I established the office of *contrôleur des deniers communs* to exercise a supervisory power over municipal finances. This policy was pursued and extended during the sixteenth century. Royal bailiffs were appointed to regulate elections, preside over municipal assemblies and scrutinize accounts (Doc. 33). The Ordinance of Moulins (1566) decreed that royal courts should take over all the towns' judicial rights in civil affairs. However a number of these regulations remained a dead letter; the towns were growing richer and the crown could not altogether afford to antagonize the rich men who controlled them (Doc. 34).[26]

The situation changed towards the end of the sixteenth century with the outbreak of the civil Wars of Religion. The authority of the king was so critically diminished that a host of separate communities rejected his dominion. A pamphleteer writing in 1593 noted, '*de degré en degré il ne se trouvera village en France qui ne se fasse Souverain*'.[27] With the re-establishment of royal authority Henry IV acted severely against the towns, modifying their constitutions, supervising their elections and imposing his own candidates, limiting their judicial powers and exacting 'gifts' of money. As the seventeenth century proceeded the crown tightened its control especially over the towns' financial organization (Doc. 35). The king's officials, the *intendants*, supervised their budgets and the urban communities finally lost the right to impose taxes and spend the resulting revenue as they wished. By Louis XIV's reign the towns were ceasing to be the semi-independent units in the state which they had been for so long (Docs. 50, 63).

[25] Olivier-Martin, *Histoire du droit Français*, p. 404.
[26] Doucet, *Les institutions de la France*, i. 366-7.
[27] G. Weill, *Les théories sur le pouvoir royal en France pendant les Guerres de Religion*, Paris 1892, p. 258.

The towns' representation in the Estates-General remained an important element, but by the sixteenth century it no longer formed the total complement of the third estate. Louis XI only convened one meeting of the Estates, at Tours in 1468. The next convocation held shortly after his death in 1484 was a milestone in the institution's development. For the first time membership of the Estates-General was organized along genuinely representative lines. Not only were previously unrepresented areas like Flanders and Dauphiné included but the election procedure was altered to take a more realistic account of social patterns. The third estate was christened at Tours in 1484 (Doc. 36)[28] The new system was complicated. The clergy and nobility of each royal bailiwick were summoned to attend meetings in the bailiwick's chief centre, there to elect some of their number to represent them in the Estates-General. The same procedure was applied to the third estate. However, it did not work very well because electors living a long way from the centre remained unrepresented. In the latter part of the sixteenth century, when the estates were enjoying a great revival of authority, the system of election was finally fixed. For the first and second estates the election procedure began immediately below bailiwick level in one of the subordinate areas of jurisdiction into which the bailiwick was divided. There all the clergy and nobles of the area were entitled to choose their delegates to go forward to the next stage, a meeting of the whole bailiwick. The third estate's representatives were chosen at parish level by the heads of each household. The representatives of all three estates were joined in the full bailiwick assembly by delegates of the towns, themselves elected by urban assemblies representing the wealthy upper layer of town society. Under the chairmanship of the royal bailiff this assembly elected from among its members those who were to proceed to the meeting of the Estates-General itself. It also formulated the various catalogues of complaints, the *cahiers de doléances*, which the three estates wished, usually separately, to bring to the king's attention (Doc. 37). Once in session the estates were entitled and expected to advise the king on whatever topics he required counsel: in 1484 it was the manner in which the regency should be conducted, in 1576 and 1588 it was the problems resulting from the introduction of protestantism into France and the effects of the religious wars (Doc. 38).

Traditionally the estates also had a role in the matter of taxation but in this sphere the role of the provincial estates begins to obtrude. Here once more one is brought up against a basic fact of political life in pre-revolutionary France, the persistence of rights and privileges founded upon custom which the crown, also for customary reasons,

[28] Lot and Fawtier, *Histoire des institutions Françaises*, ii. 573-4.

was obliged to guarantee. Thus in 1481, when Louis XI acquired Provence for the French crown, he confirmed its privileges; Francis I acted similarly towards Dombes in 1523. Indeed, whenever a town or area of country was acquired by the crown in the sixteenth and seventeenth centuries, the confirmation of its existing privileges was incorporated into the legal contract. The Treaty of the Pyrenees, signed in 1659, contained such a clause on behalf of the province of Roussillon (Doc. 39). In rare cases the king even agreed to legislate for particular areas under special titles, as Count of Provence, for example, or Dauphin of Viennois. Not all provinces had their own estates; those that had, the *pays d'états*, were mostly, though not all on the periphery of the kingdom: Brittany, Provence, Burgundy, Languedoc, Normandy, Dauphiné, Guyenne and Périgord. These estates, like the Estates-General, were normally composed of representatives from the three estates summoned in accordance with the particular custom established in each area: the nobility dominated the estates of Brittany, the bishops were prominent in those of Languedoc, and in the latter too, most unusually, peasants were eligible for election. Only the king had the authority to summon these provincial assemblies, but here again custom dictated the frequency of the meetings: the estates of Languedoc met every year, those of Brittany every other year, those of Burgundy every three years. When the session began the king's representatives—the governor or his lieutenant, the *intendant* of the locality, or members of the royal council—presented his requests, a similar procedure to that followed in meetings of the Estates-General, and then withdrew whilst the requests were debated (Doc. 40). To reach agreement a good deal of backstage negotiation was needed and the estates had groups of permanent officials or small pilot committees to work with royal officials and ensure collaboration between the three orders.[29]

Whenever they were convened the estates were allowed to draw up their catalogue of complaints to which the king would respond article by article, provided that the catalogue was not couched in threatening terms. The principal causes of dissatisfaction were violations of traditional provincial rights and liberties resulting from royal intervention, and frequently the sovereign promulgated new measures to satisfy local sensibilities (Doc. 41). But the king, too, had his reasons for convening the local estates. Around the turn of the fifteenth-sixteenth centuries they were required on a number of occasions to

[29] Olivier-Martin, *Histoire du droit Français*, pp. 396-7; Doucet, *Les institutions de la France*, i. 314-28; the most recent work on this subject has been that of J. Russell Major, *Representative Institutions in Renaissance France*, 1421-1559, Madison, Wisconsin 1960, and *The Deputies to the Estates-General in Renaissance France*, Madison, Wisconsin 1960.

ratify international treaties, a less expensive or complicated procedure than the summoning of the Estates-General. They also played an important part in establishing and preserving the customary law of their area. Their chief significance however lay in the control which they wielded over royal taxation.

The traditions of French kingship had never allowed the monarch to tax his subjects without their consent. He was expected to live off the resources of his domain and when the needs of his state outgrew those resources he had to seek approval before exacting a general levy. The later Capetians and the early Valois had employed the machinery of the Estates-General less to satisfy their fiscal needs directly than to establish a platform from which they could explain what those needs were and how they had arisen. The actual negotiations were usually conducted on a provincial level and therefore the restraining influence of the separate local estates over the king remained greater than that of the national assembly. However this influence was threatened in the mid-fifteenth century. The Hundred Years War with England imposed a heavy financial burden and the level of taxation was consequently high. Over and above the regular annual sums, the various estates were forced to vote an additional levy for the maintenance of the army. This burden was a constant cause of complaint, and after 1451, when the war was going well and the threat to the kingdom's internal security had diminished, Charles VII was able to lessen his requirements. In return for a significant reduction in overall taxation the king now began to raise money to support the army without everywhere seeking the estates' approval, and in some areas of central France, where the relief was deeply felt, the provincial assemblies ceded their right to approve taxation and disappeared in consequence. But in a number of those important localities, the *pays d'état* where the provincial estates survived, the right to vote the level of royal taxation survived too. In the period of the Italian wars under Francis I and Henry II the king's financial needs rose, and meetings of the estates became more frequent. The king respected this privilege as he did other provincial rights. For their part the estates never felt able to refuse royal requests for a *don gratuit*, though, as with the clergy's gift, there was no guarantee that the king would get all that he asked for. As was also the case with the clergy's *don gratuit*, the amount demanded by the central government tended to increase as the years passed (Docs. 40, 42). It is worth adding that even in areas unimpeded by provincial restrictions of this kind the crown's financial position still depended heavily in the seventeenth century upon the co-operation of its own local officials (Docs. 43, 60, 61).

Thus in one vital respect the provincial estates, or some of them at least, remained more powerful than the Estates-General. Although that institution enjoyed a revival in the second half of the sixteenth century and although it refused, in 1576 and 1588, to provide any financial assistance at all, the crown was still able to obtain money by other expedients. The truth of the matter was that the Estates-General had never been universally popular; after the meeting of 1484 it was not convened for a long time, partly because the crown found the results were not worth the trouble of summoning it in the first place, and partly because the decentralized particularist structure of the country frequently made provincial decisions more meaningful than national ones. The fact, therefore, that the Estates-General was not summoned between 1614 and 1789 does not betoken a change in the nature of royal government. In 1614 the three estates voluntarily accepted the crown's overriding authority after their feuding had once more demonstrated their incapacity to reach any agreement amongst themselves.[30] Henceforth the king saw no purpose in convening the estates. That seventeenth and eighteenth century attitude was no more a sign of increasing royal arbitrariness than was Charles VII's decision after 1440 to reject national in favour of provincial consultation.

There remains an important qualification to reiterate on the subject of consultative assemblies. The king was not confined either to meetings with the Estates-General or with provincial estates. He could and did convene a variety of other assemblies which might include, according to the nature of the business under discussion, royal officials, representatives of important towns, members of the *parlement* and of the University of Paris, princes of the blood and representatives of leading noble families, archbishops, bishops and abbots. All these assemblies performed the indispensable task of offering counsel to the sovereign when he required it, though none of them could trespass, nor ever presumed to do so, upon the king's obligation to take the ultimate decisions.

THE KING'S ARMY

That this sovereign authority was limited by practical as well as theoretical considerations is illustrated by an examination of the crown's relationship with the army. In the period up to the thirteenth century there was no royal army as such; in times of need the king had to negotiate for troops with his great vassals. But with the vast extension of the royal domain under Philip Augustus the king of France began to need a more reliable and permanent military force.[31] The answer lay in the introduction of money payments, and the feudal host was gradually replaced by the mercenary army. One of

[30] R. Mousnier, 'L'évolution des institutions monarchiques', pp. 58-63.
[31] Lot and Fawtier, *Histoire des institutions Françaises*, ii. 523-31.

the great problems of this system, of course, was how to control these troops who often acted as mere brigands, causing quite as much harm to their employer's interests as to those of the enemy. In 1445 Charles VII took the first important steps to fashion a royal army out of these lawless mercenary bands. At that time it numbered little more than 8,000 men, but even this number imposed a great strain on the royal exchequer; henceforth the French crown was to be involved in a losing battle to obtain sufficient funds to maintain a permanent and growing military force. The *ban et arrière-ban* continued to exist alongside the paid force though it was increasingly inefficient (Docs. 44, 45). It tended to become another royal financial expedient; in return for money the king excused his vassals' service obligation—a wise decision in every respect since he could use the money thus obtained to hire far more effective soldiers than the anachronistic feudal system could provide.

The decline of the *ban et arrière-ban* did not diminish the importance of the nobles' role in the army. The core of the royal army at the end of the fifteenth century were the *compagnies d'ordonnance*, volunteers who had to be of noble rank. Each company was under the command, usually nominal, of a great noble, often a prince of the blood. Existing side by side with the *compagnies d'ordonnance* were the *élite* forces of the *maison du roi* who formed the king's personal bodyguard and included the French and Swiss Guards, the light cavalry and the musketeers. All their members too were noblemen. The non-noble element in the French army was provided by the infantry. The fifteenth century *franc-archers*, organized on a parochial basis, were the predecessors of the foot soldiers who from the sixteenth century onwards began to outnumber the cavalry; by 1552 the French army contained over 30,000 infantrymen and under 5,000 horsemen (Doc. 45). The infantrymen were either recruited haphazardly by individual captains acting under a royal commission, or for a time they were banded into legions organized upon a strictly provincial basis: both officers and men of the Norman legion had to be natives of Normandy, and the same rule applied to the other five legions, those of Brittany, Burgundy, Dauphiné, Languedoc and Guyenne. But the legion organization, like that of the earlier *franc-archers* proved unworkable, finally breaking down during the Wars of Religion, which forced the government to undertake another experiment (Doc. 46). This was the introduction of regiments, the grouping of small bands of soldiers into much larger units under a single command. This regimental system survived the civil wars and became the established form of organization for the French infantry. To the three original regiments of Picardy, Champagne and Piedmont,

Henry IV added his own regiment of Navarre and Louis XIII a further eleven.[32]

Although the officer class was originally the preserve of the second estate—a stipulation only partly supported by the ordinance of Blois (1579)—by 1584 it was certainly possible for members of the third estate to enter the *compagnies d'ordonnance*. It was also equally true of the army, as of every other walk of life, that men of humble origins could aspire to high rank and achieve noble status in the process. The Code Michau (1629) declared that every soldier, according to the quality of his service, might aspire to the rank of captain or above (Doc. 47). The fact that certain military offices were becoming venal also helped ambitious wealthy middle-class families to enter the army at subaltern level, thus acquiring the social status which attached to a career in arms and allowing them to set out in pursuit of higher military honours and consequent entry into the second estate. Here again the pattern reveals the familiar cyclical tendency. It has been possible to establish the ancestry of 164 of Louis XIV's lieutenant-generals, and of these high ranking officers one in four belonged to families which only achived noble status during the sixteenth or seventeenth centuries.[33]

The king was bound to provide security for his realm from outside attack and to preserve law and order within his domains, tasks in which the army's role was clearly basic; yet it was not until late in the seventeenth century that the royal army could be considered firmly under the king's control. Although the king was no longer forced to negotiate with his great vassals for military assistance, he had still to depend upon the loyalty of his commanders and the readiness of his troops to obey their orders. Before the Wars of Religion the royal forces could do nothing to deter the large public gatherings of Huguenots meeting in defiance of the government and with the armed support of members of the nobility, nor could they make any impression upon the internecine struggle which followed (Doc. 48).[34]

During the Fronde, too, the king was forced to flee from his capital, and his eventual triumphant return was not the result of victory on the battlefield. A little earlier, in 1642, Louis XIII expressed his fears that if war did not shortly cease there would be no French infantry willing to continue fighting.[35]

[32] Zeller, *Les institutions de la France*, pp. 297-307.
[33] A. Corvisier, 'Les généraux de Louis XIV et leur origine sociale', in *Le dix-septième siècle*, vols XLII-XLIII, 1959, p. 41.
[34] H. G. Koenigsberger, 'The Organisation of Revolutionary Parties in France and the Netherlands during the Sixteenth Century', in *Journal of Modern History*, vol. XXVII, 1955, pp. 337-8.
[35] Marion, *Dictionnaire*, p. 23.

In the case of the major conflicts already referred to, and indeed in less widespread though nevertheless serious disturbances like the revolt of the *duc de* Montmorency in Languedoc in 1632, the king's military vulnerability was very apparent.[36] Yet these critical moments only highlighted what was in fact a perennial state of affairs, though contemporaries would not have interpreted the situation in terms of royal vulnerability. Not only was the army less than totally reliable: there was no organized police force at all. Justice, administration and police were all considered facets of a single function and all were performed by a great variety of officials and institutions whose authority varied from place to place and from time to time. Even in Richelieu's day the administration of the army was a marvel of disorganization (Doc. 49). No ruler, however fierce his attachment to strong government, could ever contemplate the sort of authority over his subjects which it has become commonplace for all governments of our own generation to exert. Yet the monarchy survived unscathed and the politically influential elements in society remained wedded to the status quo; the reason lay in the continuing invulnerability of the French crown's moral authority.

THE KING'S COUNCILLORS

To assist him in the task of governing effectively the king had at his disposal, then, a number of officials and administrators both at the centre of government and in the provinces. Reference has already been made to the royal council and its somewhat amorphous character. Not that one should be surprised at the lack of definition in this as in many other institutions of the same period. The emphasis upon systematized government only came when royal government was no longer considered part of the natural order, inspiring intuitive respect and needing no clearly defined procedures through which to make its impact felt. At the beginning of the sixteenth century the council was variously called the *conseil du roi*, the *conseil privé*, the *conseil étroit* and the *conseil d'Etat*, though before the end of the century the last phrase was the one usually employed to describe the whole institution. However, by that time the council had become a complex series of councils as another period of specialization, like that which had earlier caused the separation of the *parlement* from the *curia regis*, gathered pace. Under Francis I the *conseil des affaires* was primarily concerned with international politics and with great matters of state; it may be identified with the *conseil secret* of his immediate predecessors and the *conseil d'en haut* of the Bourbons.

---

[36] V. L. Tapié, *La France de Louis XIII et de Richelieu*, Paris 1952, pp. 368-74.

The title of *conseil d'Etat*, besides its application to the council over-all, was applied to that section which dealt with administrative matters within the kingdom. These matters were partly fiscal and partly judi-cial. Yet by the end of the sixteenth century two more specialized royal councils had emerged, also concerned with these two spheres. The first of them, the *conseil des parties*, was the king's council acting in a purely judicial capacity, a capacity which it had never lost despite the fact that both the *parlement* and the *grand conseil*, representing at different times the judicial element of the king's court, had been detached from it. The judicial role of this latest emanation was gen-erally confined to matters which for one reason or another could not readily be settled by the sovereign courts, or which had caused un-satisfactory verdicts to be given at that level. Finally the *conseil des finances* made intermittent appearances, its chief task coming at the end of the century with the urgent need to balance the royal budget.[37] In Louis XIII's reign financial matters were divided between two councils, the *conseil d'Etat et finances* and the *conseil de finances et direction*. In 1630 a new division of the council was instituted, the *conseil des dépêches*. This council was to control the interior admini-stration of the kingdom and oversee the relations between the king and the clergy, the towns and *pays d'état*. It too had a judicial capa-city and was used to withdraw controversial cases from the *parle-ments'* jurisdiction and quash controversial decrees issued by the sovereign courts.[38]

The *conseil d'Etat*, with its various sub-divisions, formed the hub of royal government. It is therefore important to discover what sort of people sat at the king's council table. To begin with, it must be particularly noted that although certain officers and dignitaries might expect to be summoned, nobody had a right to come. It was and always had been the king's prerogative to seek advice from whomever he wished. The king's immediate family might expect to be consulted and so might those men who were honoured with titles like constable, chancellor, admiral and so forth, which from the reign of Henry III became officially known as the great offices of the crown. Then there were the representatives of powerful aristocratic houses whose autho-rity was supreme in their own localities, and whose relations with the king retained something of the old spirit of *primus inter pares*, and the prelates who traditionally formed part of the king's entourage. Such people would certainly hope to command important consultative roles, and since monarchical government was personal and informal it would be very natural for the king to confide in those who were socially closest to equality with him. That is not to say that he confided ex-

[37] Doucet, *Les institutions de la France*, i. 131-52.
[38] Olivier-Martin, *Histoire du droit Français*, p. 440.

clusively in such advisers; after the accession of the first Valois that was rarely ever the case. The reason was partly because the king required expert advice especially when the council met in its judicial capacity, and partly because he knew that in the event of royal weakness his council could be used by powerful political rivals to dominate and direct royal policy. That had happened on occasion—under Philip V and Charles VI, for example, at the beginning of the fourteenth and fifteenth centuries—and the king was always anxious to break any precedent which might support an aristocratic stranglehold over the council, by asserting his right to nominate his own councillors.[39]

One long established group of councillors were the *maîtres des requêtes* (Doc. 50). These men were lawyers whose office had been closely linked in service with the king since the thirteenth century and who were employed by the sovereign in a variety of administrative roles. Their legal expertise was invaluable when the council sat in a judicial capacity. They were no less indispensable to Louis XIV than they had been to Louis XI, and in the intervening period their number had grown from a mere eight to almost ninety.[40] However the professional element in the council which assumed the greatest significance in the course of this period was the office of secretary of state. Already in the early years of the fourteenth century royal secretaries had acquired the right to sign documents on the king's authority and from that stage, granted the continuity of the crown's authority, the development of the office from a position of subordinate but considerable importance to one of complete indispensibility, was predictable enough. Henry II gave four of his secretaries the official title of *sécretaire d'Etat* and in 1561 they became full members of the *conseil des affaires*. During the Wars of Religion their fortunes were mixed, though under Henry III they were largely responsible for running the government.[41] Again in the reign of Louis XIII their influence was great. At that time too a certain amount of specialization could be discerned: the secretaries for war, for the royal household and for the various provincial areas were identifiable figures with an administrative organization backing them (Doc. 49). They were all eligible to attend all the councils save the supreme *conseil d'en Haut* though two of them, Sublet and Chavigny, were normally members of that body too. In council sessions they were free to argue their own point

[39] Lot and Fawtier, *Histoire des institutions Françaises*, ii. 578.
[40] Marion, *Dictionnaire*, pp. 358-9.
[41] The development of this office in the sixteenth century is traced by N. M. Sutherland, *The French Secretaries of State in the Age of Catherine de Medici*, London 1962.

of view and afterwards to check and even to modify the wording of proposed council decrees.[42]

Closely associated with the secretaries in the royal council were the superintendents of finance.[43] The responsibility for controlling and safeguarding the king's finances was a good deal older than the title which only took firm root towards the middle of the sixteenth century, though Briçonnet under Charles VIII and Semblançay under Francis I performed precisely that function. Sully held the office under Henry IV, and though after his disgrace it temporarily disappeared the office was re-established in 1619 and was throughout the seventeenth century considered a major political appointment. One of the superintendents' chief financial tasks was to prepare annual budgets containing estimates of revenue and expenditure for the following year. They also played a leading part in assessing the amount to be levied each year from the *taille* and in deciding upon the imposition of new taxes. In the royal council under Louis XIII and Richelieu the superintendents of finance far outweighed the secretaries of state in importance; indeed, with the chancellor they were considered the king's key advisers (Doc. 51).

The superintendents were the chief financial officials in the royal council. Below them, though also members of the *conseil d'Etat* in the sixteenth century and of almost every council in the seventeenth, came the *intendants* of finance. This office had originally been performed by *maîtres des requêtes*, but as the financial tasks with which they were charged became more specialized in the course of the sixteenth century, the *intendants* became a separate group enjoying greater prestige and importance than the other *maîtres* who advised the sovereign. In the reign of Louis XIII the number of *intendants* of finance was fixed at four.

There are several points to be made about membership of the king's councils. It is true that viewed over a period of two centuries the tendency was undoubtedly for the council to become more specialized and consequently to recruit more expert administrators. But this tendency affected neither the role of the monarch nor his authority. Even in the days of Richelieu's ascendancy the Cardinal continued to depend upon royal support for the implementation of decisions just as the king continued to expect and receive advice from his councillors (Doc. 14b). Although Richelieu dominated the council and manipulated its members in a novel fashion that fact in no way altered the nature of conciliar government which went on functioning according to the basic political principle that the king could depend for advice

[42] O. Ranum, *Richelieu and the Councillors of Louis XIII*, Oxford 1963, pp. 61-3.
[43] *Ibid.*, pp. 120-42.

upon whomever he pleased. In fact the growth of a bureaucratic conciliar system in the seventeenth century marked no sort of fundamental
change in the balance of central government which continued
to revolve around the person of the king. Richelieu himself was no
bureaucrat; his influence harked back to pre-renaissance days when
great prelates were the natural counsellors of kings. It is worth repeating that although the members of the king's council tended, especially
during the reign of Louis XIII, to become more specialized, there
was still a great deal of common ground and the departmental idea
was still subordinate. The most recent historian of that period has
commented: 'Councillors worked with great freedom on all problems
in the various sections of the Council', and again, 'A criss-cross of
duties and personnel characterizes government in the seventeenth century. . . . Studying ministerial government by offices would be arti-
ficial if it were not combined with an analysis of the other duties
carried out by the same officers in other capacities.'[44]

Turning to the social implications of these political developments
at the heart of government, the element of continuity is more striking
than might at first appear. It has already been established that nobility
in France was of two kinds, hereditary, which involved membership
of the *noblesse de race*, and personal.[45] An idea persists that there was
also a division between *noblesse de robe* and *noblesse d'épee*, robe
and sword, with the implication of the latter's social superiority over
the former, but that idea is of dubious validity (Docs. 52, 70). Both
expressions lack precise meaning. That of *noblesse d'épee* was scarcely applicable to nobility acquired as a direct result of military service, since that connection was only legally established in 1750.[46] It
is more usually intended to convey both the idea of ancient lineage, of
nobility acquired before the royal practice of selling offices greatly
increased the number of noble families, especially in the legal sphere,
and that of an exclusively military career coupled with the obligation
to live nobly between campaigns, whilst the phrase *noblesse de robe*
presumably includes not only lawyers but also administrators who
rose to prominence in the king's service in the sixteenth and seventeenth centuries. This distinction is a dangerous one. The fact of
noble status was much more important than its origins. Besides, many
lawyers and administrators came from families which were already
noble and many non-robe noblemen were related to one or other of
the great legal dynasties. Robe and sword stood for different professions, not different social levels. If members of each group possessed

[44] *Ibid.*, pp. 5, 7.
[45] *Supra.*, p. 23.
[46] J. F. Bluche, *Les magistrats du parlement de Paris au XVIIIe siècle* (1715-
1771), Paris 1960, p. 303.

hereditary nobility, they were as indistinguishably a part of the *noblesse de race* as the Great Condé himself.

A brief enquiry into the social origins of some of the leading councillors of the period illustrates the point. The most celebrated secretary of state of the sixteenth century was Nicholas de Neufville, *seigneur* of Villeroy. His grandfather had been a member of Henry II's council and his father a distinguished administrator, a knight and indisputably a member of the *noblesse de race*. Neufville was married to a daughter of another leading secretary of state, Claude de Laubespine. Laubespine came from a legal family. His father had probably been a royal secretary in his day and though his grandfather was a *bourgeois* of Orléans there was no doubting the validity of the grandson's noble status: knight, baron of Châteauneuf-sur-Cher, viscount of la Forest-Taumier, *seigneur* of Beauvoir-sur-Arnon, Hautrive, Rousson, Montgaugier and Coussières. A third secretary of state, Claude Pinart, knight, *seigneur* of Cramailles and baron of Valois profited from the patronage of Catherine de Medici to reach high office with a less promising background than either Neufville or Laubespine. These three secretaries all possessed hereditary nobility, the last two as a result of the exercise of their high office, Neufville in succession to his father's title.[47]

A similar pattern emerges from a study of Louis XIII's councillors. Claude le Bouthillier, though a nobleman by birth, was an impoverished one who with Richelieu's support rose first to the office of secretary of state and finally to that of superintendent of finance. This office he shared with Claude de Bullion. Bullion was closely connected with the legal world: his mother was a Lamoignon, one of the greatest of robe families, and he himself followed his father as a magistrate in the *parlement* of Paris. Another secretary of state, François Sublet, *seigneur* of Noyers, was also assisted in his early career by his maternal connection with the *parlementaire* world though his father was only a minor official in the *chambre des comptes*. Again, all these men were members of the *noblesse de race* though all acquired that status from different backgrounds. Bouthillier was born a nobleman; Bullion acquired personal nobility through his membership of the *parlement*, and his son, who also entered the *parlement*, would have achieved hereditary nobility according to the principle of *patre et avo consulibus* had not his father already acquired it through his administrative services to the crown; Sublet de Noyers owed his hereditary title entirely to his service in the king's councils.[48]

The king's councillors then were noblemen whatever their previous ancestry. Their families intermarried with representatives of the robe

[47] Sutherland, *The French Secretaries of State*, passim.
[48] Ranum, *Richelieu and the Councillors of Louis XIII*, passim.

and of the sword: though Laubespine's daughter was married to
Neufville, his nephew Mauvrissière was a military commander, the
governor of St-Dizier, who was himself, incidentally, a close friend of
Neufville. In the seventeenth century representatives of the Bullion
family served indiscriminately in high legal and military offices, adding to their distinguished robe connections alliances with the sword,
in the shape of the families of Crussol and Montmorency. What we
have observed is simply another turn of the social wheel by which new
men seized the opportunity in response to royal needs first to attain
hereditary nobility and then to set their families in pursuit of further
dignities and honours which they observed to be in the possession of
contemporaries who were themselves the descendants of new men too.
It is no surprise therefore to discover that Neufville's son Villeroy
became a peer and a marshal of France, that Bullion's descendants
acquired the title of marquis, and that Bouthillier's son became a
count. In these examples may be discerned the two most significant
aspects of French nobility, its distinctiveness and its accessibility.

JUDICIAL ORGANIZATION

The king with the assistance of his council had the enormous task
of co-ordinating and regulating the affairs of a large state in which the
power of the central government was strictly limited by both theoretical and practical considerations. The country's judicial organization is the natural starting point from which to examine how the task
was accomplished. Although the king kept the right to dispense justice
through his council, the normal supreme court of appeal was originally
the *parlement* of Paris.[49] At one stage, this court claimed jurisdiction
over the whole kingdom and it retained judicial control over that area
which had at first constituted the royal domain, the Ile de France and
Picardy, Champagne and Brie, Touraine and the Orléannais, Anjou
and Maine, the Auvergne, Saintonge and Poitou, Dunkirk and parts
of Burgundy. But with the expansion of royal authority and the subsequent large increase in judicial business a number of provincial
courts with sovereign powers within their own areas were set up. The
king was also anxious to respect the long established judicial traditions which existed in some of the newly acquired lands. The first of
these provincial *parlements* was established at Toulouse in 1443 with
jurisdiction over the *Midi*. In 1456 Charles VII confirmed that the
ancient court of Dauphiné, sitting at Grenoble, should also have the
title of a royal *parlement*. Next, Louis XI decided in 1467 that the areas
of Guyenne and Gascony, which immediately after their reconquest

[49] J. H. Shennan, *The Parlement of Paris*, London 1968, pp. 78-84.

from the English had been placed under the jurisdiction first of the *parlement* of Paris then of the *parlement* of Toulouse, should have their own *parlement* at Bordeaux. The *parlement* of Burgundy, sitting at Dijon, was established in 1476 shortly before the death of the last duke of Burgundy, Charles the Bold. The exchequer of Normandy was of ancient origin, and after that province's absorption into the French state it retained its sovereign court. However, the influence of the *parlement* of Paris increasingly restricted the exchequer's independence and was partly responsible for its decline as an effective organ of justice. In 1499 Louis XII reconstituted the exchequer, making it entirely independent of Paris; from the reign of his successor, Francis I, it became known as the *parlement* of Rouen. The *parlement* of Aix-in-Provence was set up in 1501, nineteen years after that province had been inherited by Louis XI, to replace the existing judicial organization of the counts of Provence. The *parlement* of Brittany was eventually constituted in 1553 after a long period of resistance from this most separatist inclined of provinces. Further *parlements* were established during the seventeenth century at Pau for Navarre in 1620 and at Metz for the three bishoprics in 1633, while three supreme councils, which were *parlements* in all but name, were set up at Arras for Artois in 1530, at Colmar for Alsace in 1657, and at Perpignan for Roussillon in 1660.

Despite the appearance of these additional sovereign courts the *parlement* of Paris remained unassailably the most important even in purely judicial terms, not only because of its seniority and the size of its area of jurisdiction, but because certain cases—those concerning the king's right of *régale* for example—continued to be settled in Paris irrespective of their place of origin, and because certain privileged individuals holding royal letters of *committimus* could take their disputes directly to the Paris *parlement*.

Once more it bears repeating that the French state was not systematized. Besides the frequent jurisdictional disputes between the *parlements* and the king's council, the former had also to contend with the rival authority of a number of other sovereign courts functioning either upon a provincial level or throughout the whole kingdom. One of them was the *chambre des comptes* which emanated from the *curia regis* and was empowered to judge in the last instance matters relating to the king's finances. Another was the *cour des aides* which had been instituted by the Estates-General in 1355 and was subsequently taken over by the crown and given the task of deciding on appeal cases involving the payment of certain taxes, including the *aides*, the *taille* and the *gabelle* (Docs. 53, 58). The *cour des monnaies* had a much more limited authority, being confined to cases arising out of the counterfeiting or devaluation of the currency, but the *grand*

conseil, the *parlements'* chief rival, had an extremely vague competence, being frequently employed by the king to settle disputes in which
he judged the *parlements'* attitude obstreperous (Doc. 42a). The jurisdiction of the *grand conseil* covered the whole kingdom but each of
the other three Parisian courts had provincial counterparts.

Below the level of these superior courts came the bailiwicks and
seneschalcies, the latter being usually though not exclusively found in
the *Midi*. The bailiwicks had jurisdiction in the first instance over
civil matters involving the nobility or royal officials, ecclesiastical benefices, most cases in which the royal domain was involved, and some
criminal matters which were added to the bailiwicks' competence by
the application of the doctrines of *prévention* and *cas royaux*. On
appeal they judged all sentences given in inferior royal jurisdictions,
prévôtés, vicomtés, châtellenies and also, in criminal cases, the verdicts of seignorial courts. Like their judicial superiors, the *parlements*,
they registered and published royal ordinances and any *parlementaire*
decrees which applied to their particular area; they also produced
administrative regulations of their own which had the force of law
provided that they were not annulled by the local *parlement*. These
regulations covered a wide range of activities: the maintenance of
order, the supply of provisions, the price of food, the election of municipal officers, the supervision of schools and hospitals, the upkeep of
fortifications, the levying of the *ban et arrière-ban*. Men of the *ancien
régime* saw no confusion between administrative and judicial duties;
they accepted that all judicial institutions, including the *parlements*,
should exercise police powers too.

Mention should also be made of the establishment in 1552 of a new
tribunal, the *présidial*, whose limited authority lay between that of
the *parlement* and the bailiwick. In criminal matters its authority
differed little from that of the bailiwick, but in civil affairs the *présidial* court judged on appeal cases settled in the bailiwick provided
that the damages involved were not more than five hundred *livres*
(Doc. 32). The new tribunal was intended to lighten the burden of
appeal which afflicted all the *parlements*, though another motive was
undoubtedly the king's desire to create a number of new saleable
offices. The royal *présidial* court was made up of nine judges, all of
them qualified lawyers, and since it has been estimated that by the
end of the sixteenth century sixty-five such courts had been established,
it may be inferred that however expeditious the processes of justice
had become as a result—and there is little evidence to suggest any
improvement in that direction—the king's exchequer had certainly
shown a profit.[50]

[50] Doucet, *Les institutions de la France*, i. 258-67.

The *parlements* and the bailiwicks both helped to consolidate the crown's essentially judicial authority and to draw the kingdom into a single corporate institution bound by the ties of the king's law. This achievement was accomplished with difficulty; for not only were there political obstacles, but the law itself varied enormously up and down the country. There were three main elements to be considered, customary, Roman and canon law. Customary law, based upon oral tradition, was originally quite likely to change with the local landscape: one law for one side of a valley, another for the opposite slope. In time, with the increase of royal prestige, customary law was to some extent integrated though only upon a provincial basis. In the fifteenth century the king took the initiative, Charles VII decreeing in his celebrated ordinance of Montils-les-Tours that the customs of the kingdom should be drawn up in writing, approved by the *parlements* and confirmed finally by the crown. The customs established in this way would then be enforced as law in the particular area from which they came. In 1497 Charles VIII refined the procedure. Henceforth a commission, usually of members of the *parlements*, after consultation at bailiwick level with the king's local legal officials and representatives of the three estates, approved a list of customs which were then promulgated by royal command. Most of the written customary laws proclaimed in this way appeared during the reigns of Louis XII and Francis I (Doc. 54). During the remainder of the sixteenth century and beyond, legal commentators compared the diverging patterns revealed in these codes, and the vision of a uniform customary law engrossed the minds of a succession of eminent jurists including Du Moulin, Coquille and Loisel. To the complicated nature of customary law must be added the influence of Roman, civil or written law which remained strong in the south of the country, leaving its mark particularly in the sphere of criminal justice, and of canon law which played an important role not least in the development of legal procedure. The *parlements* and the bailiwicks were the agents of synthesis; through their efforts the king's law was translated into the multifarious legal tongues of ancient France.[51]

The bailiff was the chief officer in the bailiwick. His was a long-established office, first appearing in the twelfth century. It was traditionally a powerful and influential appointment carrying great prestige, and consequently much sought after. The right of nomination, of course, belonged to the king but from the middle of the fifteenth century the office was increasingly venal. Sale of office was a phenomenon which became widespread in the sixteenth and seventeenth centuries but it was by no means a novel one. Royal offices were being purchased

[51] Shennan, *The Parlement of Paris*, pp. 50-6.

in the thirteenth and fourteenth centuries, and though they were usually of only moderate importance there are instances of the sale of bailiffs' offices dating from the fourteenth century.[52] Venality was closely associated with the desire for hereditary possession of office, and the sixteenth century also witnessed the rapid development of hereditary tenure, culminating in the *paulette* declaration of 1604 (Doc. 55). This piece of legislation enabled office holders to transmit their office to their heirs if they paid an annual sum to the crown equal to one sixtieth of the office's value. Yet this was not a new development either. Indeed, the office of bailiff had been founded to replace the *prévôts* whose effectiveness as royal agents had been limited in the course of the tenth and eleventh centuries by a tendency to make their offices hereditary. On the one hand was the incumbent's temptation to found a family dynasty; on the other, the king's need to tap every available source of revenue. It is not surprising therefore that royal legislation prohibiting the practice met with little success. By the end of the fifteenth century judicial and financial offices were commonly venal and hereditary and they included not only offices at the level of bailiff and below but even those of councillor in the *parlement* of Paris and the *chambre des comptes*.[53]

As a result the character of the bailiffs' office changed. It became an honorific distinction still held in high regard, usually occupied by a representative of a distinguished noble family, but no longer a meaningful part of the judicial system. The bailiffs were rarely trained in the law and were quite incapable therefore of dealing with the legal complexities once implicit in their office. Their judicial role was taken over by subordinates. The *lieutenant-général* appeared first during the fourteenth century and he was joined in the sixteenth century by a *lieutenant-criminel* and often by a number of additional lieutenants. These men were lawyers trained to carry out the tasks which originally had been the bailiffs' responsibility (Doc. 54). By the middle of the sixteenth century these offices too had become venal and were themselves providing a means of advancement for aspiring families.[54] A number of members of the *parlement* of Paris in the eighteenth century, the Chevaliers, for example, and the Durands, were the descendants of men who had possessed one or other of these offices. It was the same story with the offices of the *présidial* courts. Two of the most famous ministerial families of the seventeenth

[52] Doucet, *Les Institutions de la France*, i. 406

[53] The standard French work on this subject is R. Mousnier, *La vénalité des offices sous Henri IV et Louis XIII*, Rouen 1945; there is also an article by G. Pagès, 'La vénalité des offices dans l'ancienne France', in *Revue historique*, vol. CLXIX, 1932, pp. 477-95.

[54] Doucet, *Les institutions de la France*, i. 255.

and eighteenth centuries, the Phélypeaux and the Turgot, who between them gave France a chancellor and a dozen secretaries of state, including the great physiocrat Turgot de Brucourt, owed their illustrious names in the beginning to two *présidial* court officers, both employed around the year 1560, at Blois and Caen respectively (Doc. 56).

Of course membership of the *parlement* of Paris and of the other sovereign courts implied high social status, the precise nature of which requires further discussion. The office of judge in a supreme tribunal involved passing judgement upon the social *élite*, and inevitably therefore these men acquired great prestige simply through the exercise of their professional duties. In a late fourteenth-century collection of written customs, the *Somme Rurale*, it was asserted that the profession of barrister conferred a dignity equivalent to that bestowed by knighthood; the principle was even more applicable to supreme court judges. There can be no doubt that they possessed at least personal nobility and, since the hereditary principle was fast gaining ground during the late fifteenth century, that personal status was frequently converted into membership of the *noblesse de race* in the third generation. Indeed, by the middle of the seventeenth century most supreme court members were granted the privilege of *noblesse de race* immediately upon taking up office. In examining the personnel of these courts the pattern which emerges, like that at bailiwick level, is of the constant rise of new families, moving out of the third and into the second estate. Nor does the growth of venality drastically alter the pattern: the social origins of sixteenth- and seventeenth-century judges were not different from those of their fifteenth-century predecessors, and despite the hereditary principle it remained possible even in the eighteenth century for new men to establish new dynasties. Like the members of the king's council, the sovereign court nobility, besides marrying within their own legal and administrative circles, were also allied with ancient military families like the La Rochefoucaulds, the Boulainvilliers and the Choiseuls.[55]

FINANCIAL ORGANIZATION

The king in Paris was also at the centre of a complicated financial organization. The medieval idea that the king should live off his domain persisted throughout the period and helped to explain the distinction made until Francis I's reign between *finances ordinaires* —revenues emanating from the king's patrimonial rights—and *finances extraordinaires*, which were taxes raised throughout the kingdom.

[55] J. F. Bluche, *L'origine des magistrats du parlement de Paris au XVIIIe siècle*, Paris 1956, is a mine of genealogical information.

D

The money exacted from the domain came from ground rents, from the sale of wood and from a variety of other seignorial dues; by the end of the fifteenth century this source was yielding only a fifth of the crown's total revenue. The administrative units through which this part of the revenue was collected were the bailiwicks and seneschalcies, and in this particular capacity the bailiffs were immediately subordinate to officials called *Trésoriers de France*. There were four of these officials under Charles VII though with the acquisition of new provinces their number had grown by the end of the century, and together they formed a central committee with responsibility for all financial matters within the ambit of the king's domain. Where extraordinary revenues were concerned the administrative units were the *élections*, not the bailiwicks, areas corresponding closely to the diocesan divisions of France (Doc. 57). The king's chief financial representative in the *élection* was the *élu* and he, like the bailiff, possessed judicial power, although his authority was limited to the right to try in the first instance cases concerning '*toutes levées de deniers imposées ou à imposer*'.[56] The alliance of judicial with administrative authority has already been referred to, and this instance further underlines the essentially judicial nature of monarchic government. The fact that two distinct organizations were superimposed on each other in this way, and that suits arising out of the levying of the *gabelle* were cognizable not before the *élu* but before another official, the *grenetier*, underlines the lack of system which was also characteristic of French government in this period, and helps to explain the rivalry which existed between jurisdictions. Appeals from both these officials were heard in the *Cour des Aides* (Docs. 26(b), 58). The *élus* in their turn were subordinate to the *Généraux des Finances* whose areas of jurisdiction, the *généralités*, coincided exactly with those of the *trésoriers*; *généraux* and *trésoriers* were admitted to the royal council where they formed a sort of collective financial ministry.

The extraordinary revenues were headed by the *taille*, strictly speaking the only direct tax, though with the passage of time additional direct levies were demanded. The *taille* was not a fixed tax; the total amount to be collected each year was decided in the king's council and then broken down into *généralités*. Each general of finance subsequently divided his allotment between his *élections*. There was a distinction between the *taille personnelle* and the *taille réelle*. The former was exacted only from unprivileged individuals, and this meant not merely that the nobility and the clergy did not pay but also that a large number of members of the third estate were also immune. Exemption from the *taille personnelle* was accorded to the king's household servants, to a variety of royal officials, members of the

[56] Zeller, *Les institutions de la France*, p. 282.

sovereign courts, royal secretaries, *élus*, members of universities including the students, barristers, notaries, mayors and aldermen, whole towns even—Normandy alone included nine such privileged communities. There were in addition a number of favoured individuals and groups, including for example the widows of men who had themselves enjoyed this privilege and communities living under the patronage of a powerful local *seigneur*. The *taille réelle* was confined to the *Midi* and the south-west. It was a less arbitrary system than the *taille personnelle* in that it was less amenable to exemption. The levy was on land rather than on the individual and though it applied only to land classified as *roturier* it was exacted from the owners irrespective of whether they were members of the first, second or third estate.

Yet any attempt to define the organization of the *taille* too closely invites misunderstanding, for almost its chief characteristic was its lack of coherence and system, something which, though no doubt irritating for those responsible for running the state's finances, was nevertheless universally accepted as fundamental to French monarchical government. Not only was the *taille* levied on two quite different bases, one of them subject to a long list of exemptions, it was levied according to special rules in one of the four *généralités*, that of Languedoc. Languedoc was also a *pays d'états*, and the estates played a part with the king's officials in assessing the tax which in that particular *généralité* was not called the *taille* but was collected under two forms, the *aide* and the *octroi*. The more peripheral *pays d'états*, on the other hand, not long incorporated into the kingdom, like Brittany and Provence, remained outside the organization altogether. Their estates voted an annual sum—known in both of these provinces as the *fouage*—which was their equivalent of the *taille*. Finally, there was the method of assessment itself which was highly arbitrary. In the first place the percentage divisions between *généralitiés* and then between *élections* were made without reliable information and apparently were altered only when inequality became overwhelmingly discernible. The subsequent sub-division into parishes was more fairly based upon information collected by the *élus* during a series of circuits (*chevauchées*) through their *élections*, though in those *pays d'états* like Guyenne and Gascony which no longer possessed a degree of financial autonomy but which were not *pays d'élections* either, this process too, in the words of a leading authority on the sixteenth century, 'reposait sur des impressions plutôt que sur des statistiques....'[57]

With all its inconsistencies the *taille* represented the greatest single source of revenue for the crown, and the amount derived from this source grew steadily. Louis XI fixed the *taille* at over four and a half

[57] Doucet, *Les institutions de la France*, ii. 565.

million *livres*; Mazarin pushed it up to fifty-five million. In addition, account must be taken of extra levies like the *taillon* which both supplemented the original levy and further complicated financial administration.

There were a variety of indirect taxes which may be grouped under three headings, *aides*, *gabelle* and customs duties. The *aides* present problems of definition which make the organization of the *taille* appear straightforward and uniform by comparison. The tax originated in the fourteenth century as one of twelve *deniers* per *livre* (about 5 per cent) upon all goods sold in the north and centre of the kingdom. From the reign of Louis XI the number of commodities subject to this tax was greatly reduced and the old division between the zones '*où les aides ont cours*' and '*où les aides n'ont pas cours*' began to disappear. Increasingly the *aides* were levied only on the sale of fish, meat, wood and principally on the sale of wine. A number of separate *aides* were added to the original at different times: the *cinq sols* of 1561, the *annuel* of 1632, the *subvention* of 1640.[58] None of these were enforced uniformly and there were lists of privileged groups enjoying exemption—clerics and noblemen in so far as the produce of their own estates was concerned, royal secretaries and members of the *cours des aides* at Paris and Rouen, the twin centres of the original area '*où les aides ont cours*'. Those *pays d'états* which had been added to France after the inauguration of the *aides* and whose estates retained financial authority, raised their own indirect taxes, handing over a proportion to the central government. The *gabelle*, though the word applied indiscriminately in the later middle ages to indirect taxes in general, came to be associated solely with the tax on salt.[59] An examination of how this tax was applied again reveals the familiar pattern of diversity. There was a novel factor at work in this case, however: some provinces produced a surfeit of salt while others produced none at all. It followed therefore that quite different arrangements would be required in each area. The *pays de grandes gabelles* in the north and centre of France constituted the greater part of the kingdom, corresponding to those areas unoccupied by the English when the tax was first introduced in the fourteenth century. Within this area, all salt had to be delivered to royal store-houses, or *greniers*, where it remained until it had dried sufficiently to be sold. At that stage the general of finances of the *généralité* concerned, fixed the sale price, making allowance both for the merchant's profit and for the king's. However, it was not difficult to bypass the *greniers* and sell salt illicitly. In an attempt to prevent this happening, French kings began to make the purchase of salt—and therefore the payment of

[58] Marion, *Dictionnaire*, pp. 9-12.
[59] Doucet, *Les institutions de la France*, ii. 577-87.

the accompanying tax—obligatory. Louis XII greatly extended this practice and Francis I tried unsuccessfully to make it universal throughout France.

Next came the *pays de petites gabelles*, the south-eastern provinces including Languedoc, Provence and Dauphiné. Salt was widely produced in these areas and it was impossible to effect as rigorous a control over its production and sale as was possible in the north. The organization, which included an extra official, the *visiteur-général* to supervise the running of the *greniers*, was finally established in a series of royal ordinances at the close of the fifteenth century. Then there was the area of the south-west, from Poitou to the Spanish border, where the influence of the central government was less than it was in the south-east. When Francis I attempted to introduce a universal *gabelle* it was in this part of the country that he met the fiercest resistance, so that his successor, Henry II, was forced to grant these lands (henceforth known as the *pays rédimés*) exemption from the *gabelle* in return for the payment of a lump sum. There were other provinces in which the *gabelle* was not supposed to be levied: Flanders, Artois, Béarn, Hainault, Navarre and chief of all, Brittany (cf. Doc. 42b). There were also numerous exemptions within the areas in which the tax was raised. Certain localities within both the *pays de grandes et petites gabelles* paid less than standard tax, the towns of Paris and Arles, for example, while individuals could acquire exemption through the privilege of *franc-salé*, a privilege widely granted to members of the first and second estates, royal councillors and secretaries and magistrates in the sovereign courts (Doc. 59).

Finally, there were the customs dues levied on goods entering or leaving the kingdom or moving across certain provincial boundaries. Once more the pattern was complicated by the fact that newly acquired provinces had generally been accorded the right to maintain their own customs arrangements. Although some moves towards uniformity were made in the reigns of both Henry II and Henry III, the Estates-General was still complaining in 1614 of the diversity of customs barriers, and half a century later Colbert was faced with the same problem.

The traditional distinction between the resources emanating from the royal domain and the so-called extraordinary levies never altogether disappeared though the king was increasingly dependent upon extraordinary revenues for his day to day needs. In the early sixteenth century a series of reforms in the king's financial administration were initiated.[60] In 1523 Francis I established a new central Treasury, the *Trésor de l'Epargne* into which all his revenues, whatever their origin, were to be indiscriminately deposited. With this reform

[60] Zeller, *Les institutions de la France*, pp. 284-90.

begaii the decline of the treasurers and generals who had between them dominated financial policy-making at royal council level. Henceforth their role was to become local and relatively insignificant. In 1543 Francis established sixteen *recettes générales*, financial and administrative divisions which replaced the original four *généralités*; henceforth these were the *généralités* and their number gradually increased from sixteen to twenty-three by the time of Louis XIV's accession. In each *généralité* a collector-general (*receveur-général*) was appointed with responsibility for the collection of all royal revenues, ordinary and extraordinary, within his area, and with authority over the collectors of particular royal revenues. In 1551 a treasurer-general was added, followed by a second and a third in 1571 and 1576. From 1577 the *Bureaux des Finances* made their appearance as the supervisory financial body in each *généralité*, composed of the collector-general and a number of treasurers (Doc. 60).

The treasurers, like the *élus* before them, were chiefly occupied with the task of periodically touring their territory, surveying, noting, inquiring into matters concerning both the king's seignorial rights and his extraordinary revenues. Like the *élus* and the bailiffs, these treasurers also possessed judicial powers, usually in matters of appeal from the *élu* (Doc. 61). That official continued to make his annual circuits to assess how the *taille* should be shared out, acting as the delegate of the treasurers and communicating with the tax-gatherers who were elected by their own communities at parish level. The bailiffs, whose authority over ordinary revenue had disappeared in the course of the financial reorganization, also found themselves in rivalry with the treasurers in other administrative spheres. At the centre, to replace the four treasurers and generals who had formed the chief financial committee, the king appointed *intendants* of finance from amongst whom emerged the superintendent whose office was to become such a prominent and powerful one during the seventeenth century.[61]

At the opposite end of the scale there was the actual collecting to be arranged, a task which the government solved increasingly by the practice of tax-farming. By this system the king authorized an individual to collect and retain a particular royal tax in lieu of prior payment to the king of an approximately equivalent sum (Doc. 53). The financier was satisfied with the arrangement because he could exact rather more than he had paid out and thus make a profit, and the king was satisfied because he received his money without the administrative problems and expense involved in collecting the tax. This system at first involved the employment of a great number of small-time businessmen

---

[61] *Supra*, p. 41; for a detailed examination of the treasurers' role, see J. P. Charmeil, *Les trésoriers de France à l'époque de la fronde*, Paris 1964.

operating in limited areas, but during the sixteenth century the number of *traitants* or *partisans*, as they were called, diminished as the areas farmed out by the king became larger. Thus in 1578 the collection of the salt tax throughout those areas known as the *pays de grandes gabelles* was entrusted by the government to a single organization and at about the same time the *Cinq Grosses Fermes* appeared, another private organization responsible for the collection of five royal impositions over a large area of central France. This tendency towards fewer and larger bodies of *traitants* continued in the seventeenth century and the financiers' unpopularity grew both with the tax-payers who felt that they were contributing money to the tax-farmers and not to the king, and with the government which was well aware of the possibilities for extortion and profiteering inherent in the system (Docs 62, 67(b), 71). Yet the latter needed the money and in the last resort was forced to rely upon the tax-farmers to provide it. Eventually in the eighteenth century, with the major exception of the *taille*, the whole kingdom became a single unit, ruled in the matter of tax-collection by little more than a score of wealthy financiers, the farmer-generals, who represented the culmination of the tax-farming principle.[62] A financial background was often the means to quick social elevation. There is no more spectacular example than that provided by the Hénault family which only achieved noble status in 1692 with the acquisition of an office of royal secretary yet two generations later was represented by the brilliant President Hénault, magistrate, author, literary celebrity and an intimate friend of Louis XV's Queen, Maria Leczinska.[63]

One other royal official concerned with the king's finances remains to be mentioned—the *intendant*—who, despite much recent valuable research, remains a shadowy figure. In the period under discussion, the *intendant* was not, of course, the important figure which he was to become in the late seventeenth and eighteenth centuries, but his was already a formidable and controversial office, virtually abolished during the first Fronde, in 1648, as a result of the antipathy aroused by his activities. On one level it is easy to account for this antipathy: the *intendants* were not, at least in the beginning, natives of the area in which they worked. They were sent in by the king as strangers to perform a variety of tasks, and their presence struck a discordant note. The *élus* and the treasurers on the other hand, and the lieutenants in the bailiwicks, were local men whose role may not have been popular but whose names and families were well known. In addition the authority of these intruding royal agents was extremely vague and apparently becoming limitless (Doc. 50). In a recent article Dr Buis-

[62] Ellul, *Histoire des institutions*, pp. 504-5.
[63] Bluche, *L'origine des magistrats*, pp. 211-12.

seret has outlined some of the activities in which some agents of
Henry IV were involved.[64] They included the supervision of financial
matters, the close surveillance of dissident elements in the provinces,
the task of representing the king at the meetings of provincial estates
and of advising him about a whole host of local problems, fiscal, military and administrative. Sometimes their task was judicial, involving a
punitive expedition to an area in which a particular law was being
flagrantly ignored. Not surprisingly, local officials and bodies resented
losing their authority, however temporarily (Doc. 63). As the seventeenth century progressed both the powers of the *intendants* and the
duration of their commissions continued to expand. Whereas originally their work had been performed in the course of a tour
through one or more provinces, it now began to appear that they
intended to reside permanently in their area of jurisdiction. Their
powers became more authoritarian. Not only could they make
decisions about virtually any affairs which interested the government—especially taxation matters—but their decisions could not be
modified, save by the intervention of the king himself. As the importance of the *intendants* increased their enemies became more
vociferous, and in the late 1620s the king agreed to concede some
points to the opposition. Henceforth, the *intendants* were not to be
resident officials and their judicial decisions were to be subject to
appeal in the courts. The animosity against them continued, however, culminating in their temporary eclipse during the Fronde.[65]
Then the opposition of the *parlement* of Paris was the decisive
factor and its opposition derived chiefly from the belief that the
intendants were still not answerable before the law for their actions,
but represented an attempt by the government to circumvent the
normal legal processes, an attitude reflected in the complaints of
provincial *parlements* (Doc. 64).[66]

On another level, however, the unpopularity of the *intendants*
seems less explicable. There was nothing novel about the idea of
sending out royal agents to enforce the king's will, provided that
what was to be enforced did not contravene the law applicable in
the area concerned. The kingdom's sense of unity depended upon
the maintenance of monarchical authority, and the king could only
exercise that authority by delegation. For centuries he had deleg-
ated his judicial power to the magistrates of his supreme court of

[64] D. J. Buisseret, 'A Stage in the Development of the French *Intendants*:
the Reign of Henry IV' in *Historical Journal*, vol. 9, 1966, pp. 27-38.

[65] Ellul, *Histoire des institutions*, pp. 486-7; R. Mousnier, 'Recherches sur
les syndicats d'officiers pendant la Fronde', in *Le dix-septième siècle*, vol. XLII-
XLIII, 1959, pp. 78-88.

[66] Shennan, *The Parlement of Paris*, p. 266.

parlement, and they, in the course of the *enquête* procedure, had travelled all over the kingdom holding local enquiries to ascertain the truth in civil actions brought before the king's tribunal. The *intendants* too were judges, not only because they were usually professionally qualified *maîtres des requêtes*, but also because they were the delegates of the supreme judicial authority in the state, the monarch. Thus they quite properly judged administrative, financial and military affairs, secure in the knowledge that their authority was properly constituted, and ignorant, as was everybody else, of the idea of separating judicial from executive power. The all-pervading nature of their mandate, therefore, and the fact that their authority frequently overshadowed that of other officials, need not appear unusual: the *élus* and the treasurers were primarily financial officials but they had judicial parts to play as well, and enough has already been said about the lack of order or system in French government to make it seem at least likely that the powers of the *intendants* should coincide in one way or another with those of a previously constituted authority.

Seen in this light the opposition, especially of the sovereign court officers in 1648, might appear unreasonable. After all, they themselves owed their authority to precisely the same sort of royal delegation and could scarcely maintain therefore that the king was acting illegally in exercising this power. In fact neither the magistrates nor the king was seeking to effect a revolution, for both sides accepted the basic tenets of monarchical government. The tension arose first out of the increasing fiscal requirements of the central government which posed threats to ancient personal and local liberties, in which context the *intendant* figured most prominently (Docs. 19, 21(b)), and secondly—and perhaps more importantly—it arose out of the deeply felt French tradition that the king, no matter what he was empowered to do, should refrain from abusing accepted legal rights and procedures. The appearance of the *intendants* is customarily and mistakenly interpreted as an indication of a new movement, leading the monarchy along the road to absolutism. In fact the movement was very much as before, less forward than cyclical, ending in a situation which was far from novel. By the eighteenth century the *intendants* were beginning to represent the needs of their administrative localities to the king rather than vice-versa—a tendency, incidentally, which one or two of them had revealed as early as the beginning of the seventeenth century.[67] They were beginning to establish local links so that, like the *élus*, the treasurers and the officials of the bailiwicks and *présidial* courts before them, their names, if not their occupation

[67] Buisseret, 'A Stage in the Development of the French *Intendants*,' p. 30.

reassured the provincial society in which they moved and with which they were becoming identified.

The *intendant's* status in society rose steadily. The first *intendants* were usually *maîtres des requêtes*, eminent lawyers whose office guaranteed them at least personal nobility, though mostly they were already hereditary nobles. The tendency already noted in members of the sovereign courts and of the royal councils towards inter-marriage with aristocratic families of robe and sword was common also to the *intendants*, and certainly there was no social antagonism between these men and the magistrates who opposed them so vehemently at the time of the Fronde. On the contrary, individual members of a family might well represent both camps. A striking illustration is provided by Jean Bochart de Saron who became first president of the *parlement* of Paris in 1628, having previously held the office of *intendant* of Poitiers. Denis Feydeau de Brou entered the *parlement* as a counsellor in 1654 and later became *intendant* of Rouen, and Louis Le Fèvre de Caumartin de Boissy who had been a counsellor in the *parlement* during the critical years of the Fronde became the *intendant* for Champagne in 1667 (Doc. 65). Henri Lambert d'Herbigny was a counsellor in the *parlement* in 1650 and *intendant* of Dauphiné in 1679; his son, a counsellor in the *parlement* of Metz and then of Paris, married the daughter of a marquis and governor of Dunkirk. The family was also related by marriage to the ancient house of Rochechouart, whose nobility could be traced back with certainty as far as the year 980.[68] Examples like these could be multiplied, and they demonstrate the repetitive element in French social history, the gradual absorption of new men into the old order.

The same process was at work at a lower level, among the financial officers whose work has already been discussed, the treasurers and the *élus*.[69] Between the two offices ran a very important line of demarcation: the treasurers' rank was the first stage in the process of ennoblement, guaranteeing personal nobility, while the office of *élu* represented the top echelon of the third estate. During the civil disturbances of the Fronde both groups showed signs of great discontent, inspired chiefly by the increasing intervention of the *intendants*. Their resentment was due both to the diminution of prestige and authority which was the inevitable result of the *intendants'* appearance and the concurrent financial losses involved. As far as the latter was concerned it is easy to exaggerate the situation. Certainly the

[68] Bluche, *L'origine des magistrats*, pp. 231-2.
[69] P. Goubert, 'Les officiers royaux des présidiaux, bailliages et élections dans la société Française au XVIIe siècle' in *Le dix-septième siècle*, vols XLII-XLIII, 1959, pp. 57-70.

value of their offices was reduced by the creation, in the course of
Louis XIII's reign, of a large number of additional offices, and some
fees formerly accruing to the *élus* and the treasurers were now find-
ing their way into the *intendants'* pockets. Yet the financial rewards
of office were not so important—as with most other venal legal
offices in France they were less a source of wealth than a sign that
the holder had already acquired it. By the middle of the seventeenth
century, an *élu* would not pay very much less than 10,000 *livres*
for his office and his financial return on this investment was not likely
to be high. On the other hand, the social prestige thus acquired was
certainly considerable. In other words, these men were already
ascending the social ladder: their families had made their money
perhaps as barristers or traders or *bourgeois* in a thriving town and
were now straddling the line between the second and third estates.
Their antipathy towards the *intendants* was primarily a matter of
injured pride, of frustrated social ambition. Thus in 1648 representatives of the treasurers and *élus* addressed a circular to their
colleagues in the following terms: '... *nos fonctions ne nous sont
points rendues et il ne nous reste plus qu'une qualité dénuée de
tout son emploi et de ce qui la rendait considérable avant le
déplorable temps où nous sommes....*'[70] Nevertheless, there is no
evidence that these officers played an active part in the Fronde, nor
that they sought to challenge the king's authority. Indeed, it would
seem unlikely that they should do so: it is one thing for an ambitious
man to show signs of frustration at an unexpected setback in his
career, but quite another for him to contemplate undermining the
social order which gave that career relevance. Those families seeking further advancement would hope in time to be absorbed into
the first or second estate; for some that would be sufficient, for
others there were even greater honours to be picked. The process
was considered normal and unexceptional. Thus the great eighteenth
century magisterial house of Bèze, whose best-known representative
was the Protestant theologian, Theodore de Bèze, reached the rank of
élu at the beginning of the seventeenth century and membership of the
parlement of Paris at the beginning of the eighteenth (Doc. 66). Similarly, the controller of finance during Louis XV's minority, Le Pelletier
de la Houssaye, included amongst his ancestors an *élu* at Mantes
in the reign of Henry IV. A treasurer at Tours under Louis XIII,
Le Febvre de la Faluère, initiated a noble line which would include
a first president of the *parlement* of Brittany. Another illustrious
family, the Le Peletier, which produced a controller of finance under
Louis XIV and was allied by marriage with the ancient family of

---

[70] Mousnier, 'Recherches sur les syndicats d'officiers', p. 85.

Montmorency, owed its fortune to a treasurer at Grenoble in the 1630s.[71]

THE GOVERNORS

There was yet one more administrative layer which played a part in the state's provincial organization, the office of governor.[72] The governor's role was primarily a military one but it was not simply that, and the problem of defining precisely what it was is not easily solved. Again, one is up against the characteristic lack of system. From the thirteenth century French kings had been in the habit of appointing supernumerary administrators above the permanent officials, the bailiffs, not on a permanent basis but with overriding authority in their areas: the fact that they tended to appear at moments of national crisis, in particular during the Hundred Years War, underlines the essentially military nature of their brief. In the closing years of the fifteenth century their authority was in fact limited to military matters: affairs of finance and justice which had come within their purview in the previous century were removed from their competence and they were charged only with commanding the king's troops and organizing the defence of the kingdom within the group of bailiwicks over which each governor presided. However, that state of affairs changed again during the sixteenth century, though perhaps it would be more accurate to admit that the office and attributes of governor were so fluid as to render any definition immediately suspect. Any royal nominee operating in one or several provinces above the level of bailiff might be called a governor. At the beginning of the sixteenth century the number of governments or provinces—these terms too could include a variety of different administrative areas—in which the governor was a well-established officer, corresponded well enough with the frontier areas where military priorities were high, but Francis I complicated matters further by appointing governors in Anjou (1516), Auvergne (1523) and Poitou (1528), and not all of these appointments seemed relevant to military needs. Throughout the remainder of the century their role remained rather vague (Doc. 42b). Though their nomination by the king was in the form of a simple commission which could be revoked at will, at least partly because the governors were invariably the representatives of extremely elevated noble houses—before his accession Francis I himself had been governor of Guyenne—the tendency to look upon the office as a permanent family appointment persisted. Thus the Guise established themselves in Burgundy and Champagne, the Condé in

---

[71] Bluche, L'origine des magistrats, passim.
[72] Doucet, Les institutions de la France, i. 229 et seq.

Picardy, the Albret in Guyenne and the Bourbon in Languedoc. Though their letters of provision insisted upon their military role, the protection of strategic areas and places, the administration of the army, the establishment of garrisons, the problems of military discipline and the maintenance of order, they frequently also included vague admonitions to act in whatever other ways were necessary for the well-being of the kingdom. Thus in a phrase the military governor was given the opportunity of becoming a military dictator. This equivocal situation becomes doubly ambiguous in reference to the crucial sphere of the governor's judicial rights. Sometimes he was considered as an agent responsible for the execution of judgments arrived at through the proper legal machinery, sometimes he was endowed with the right to demand support from the sovereign courts in his area in the implementation of his own judicial decisions.

Yet there was nothing especially remarkable about this situation: disputed areas of jurisdiction between royal officials were common enough during this period, and the essentially judicial nature of the king's office meant that the governors, like the *intendants* and the *élus*, possessed an authority as royal delegates which was judicial as well as administrative (Doc. 35). Certainly if they chose or were instructed to exercise their judicial powers outside the normal procedures in force in their localities, they would meet powerful opposition from the established tribunals, which maintained that if the king's authority was to be respected it had to eschew any appearance of arbitrariness or irregularity. The *parlements* in particular kept a watchful and often jaundiced eye upon the powers of the governors. What altered the situation was the breakdown of royal authority and with it the coming of civil war. The governors belonged to the most powerful noble houses in France, and the introduction of Calvinism into the country, coinciding with the end of the Italian wars and the sudden death of the strong king, Henry II, gave them the opportunity to exploit their enormous influence and authority to the full and act as sovereigns in their own provinces. Before the Wars of Religion the governors, like the bailiffs, tended to act only in an honorary capacity whilst their functions were taken over by a lieutenant, assisted by a council and by a captain-general who fulfilled the governor's military role. With the outbreak of war, however, the governors became resident once more. Now they controlled the provinces, promulgating ordinances, nominating important officials, seizing royal revenues, raising armies, defying the crown whose unifying grip over the country was progressively loosened. In Brittany the *duc de* Mercoeur established a virtually independent state which only returned to the royal fold in 1598.

In re-establishing royal authority Henry IV was faced with the

crucial task of curtailing the governors' powers. During the Wars
of Religion France came nearer to revolution than she was ever to
do again before 1789, though ironically it was not the governors
or their aristocratic followers who were the real revolutionaries. That
role belonged to the middle-class core of the Catholic League especially in Paris, mostly either clerics or professional men, who set up
in the capital a Committee of Sixteen which in many respects fore-
shadowed the pattern, even the vocabulary, of the Revolution.[73] But
the traditional social fabric held firm, and with the accession of
Henry IV and the promise of a renewal of firm monarchy the aristocratic element reacted strongly in favour of the established order:
the king's authority legitimately and forcefully exercised was still the
most powerful element in politics and in society. Thus Henry's task
was greatly simplified and he succeeded in limiting the governors'
powers in a way which his undistinguished predecessors had tried
in vain, that is by appointing lieutenants to keep a close watch over
their activities on the king's behalf (Doc. 42c). In addition Henry
sometimes appointed *intendants* to act as a further check, but he
did not take away from the governors the authority which was traditionally theirs, the command of the king's army (Docs. 44, 49).
Under Richelieu the power of the governors was further controlled;
the Cardinal followed Henry IV's policy of appointing his own representatives to oversee them but he also dismissed a number altogether,
something which Henry had not done.[74] Yet although the governors
never again achieved the importance that was theirs during the Wars
of Religion, they remained prominent figures, by no means confined
to an honorary role. In the unsettled decade before the Fronde their
areas of responsibility remained separate from and unco-ordinated
with the departments of the secretaries of state, and they played as
important a role as the *intendants* in controlling the spasmodic uprisings of those years (Doc. 67). The name of Condé was as closely
associated with the governorship of Burgundy in the eighteenth
century as it had been with Picardy in the sixteenth.

A SEVENTEENTH-CENTURY CRISIS?

In recent years historians have become deeply concerned with problems of seventeenth century French history. It has become fashion-
able to talk about a seventeenth-century crisis, not only in France
but throughout Europe. In a brilliant essay published in 1954, Mr
E. J. Hobsbawm commented, 'It will be generally agreed that the

[73] Koenigsberger, 'The Organisation of Revolutionary Parties', p. 349.
[74] Tapié, *La France de Louis XIII et de Richelieu*, p. 195; Marion, *Dictionnaire*,
p. 260.

seventeenth century was one of social revolt both in western and eastern Europe. This clustering of revolutions has led some historians to see something like a general social-revolutionary crisis in the middle of the century.'[75] Some five years later, Professor Trevor-Roper produced his now famous article on the general crisis of the seventeenth century to which Professor Roland Mousnier, the most eminent contemporary French historian of the period, responded critically, though fully accepting the article's basic assumption: '. . . there was a general crisis in the seventeenth century. I have discussed this crisis in various books and articles published since 1945 . . . as far back as 1953, I devoted the second part of the fourth volume of the *Histoire générale des civilisations* to the European crisis of the seventeenth century.'[76] Against such a weight of informed opinion it would seem temerity to utter a dissenting note, were it not for the fact that there is as much disagreement about the nature and causes of this crisis as there is agreement about its existence. If the solutions continue to seem inadequate the possibility must be faced that the problem they purport to solve—that of the seventeenth century crisis—may itself be illusory. In order to pursue that line of thought further it is necessary first to examine the conflicting arguments and conclusions in so far as they concern one country, France.

The marxist argument seems the most suitable point of departure, not because it is the most convincing nor the most easily demolished, but because it was a Soviet historian who first sparked off the controversy in France. Boris Porchnev published his volume, *Les soulèvements populaires en France de 1623 à 1648*, in 1948, and the original Russian edition was translated into French in 1963. Whilst drawing particular attention to the uprisings in the first half of the seventeenth century, Porchnev acknowledges that there were also popular movements during the Wars of Religion and in the period 1520 to 1550. One might add that there were even earlier insurrections like the peasant revolts in Champagne and Picardy in the mid-fourteenth century. The question is whether all these popular outbursts were of the same kind. In one way they certainly were: all of them contained an element of desperation forced upon the participants by grievous financial hardship. In that respect much of Porchnev's argument is convincing and quite unaffected by ideo-

[75] E. J. Hobsbawm, 'The General Crisis of the European Economy in the Seventeenth Century', in *Past and Present*, vol. 5, 1954, p. 37.

[76] H. R. Trevor-Roper, 'The General Crisis of the Seventeenth Century', in *Past and Present*, vol. 16, 1959, pp. 31-62; R. Mousnier, 'Discussion of H. R. Trevor-Roper: The General Crisis of the Seventeenth Century', *ibid.*, vol. 18, 1960, p. 19.

logical preoccupations. He emphasizes, for example, how government officials, like the *intendant* of Dauphiné in 1644 were reporting the misery of the local population afflicted alike by harsh taxes and crop failures (Doc. 68). The situation was made harder to bear by the growing costs of the Thirty Years War and by unfavourable economic circumstances. Unlike the previous century, the seventeenth produced great fluctuations in prices which made life doubly uncertain for those who lived close to the subsistence level. Few years passed without serious famine in one part of the country or another, and in 1629–30 and 1648–51 the whole country fell victim.[77]

But from these observations Porchnev draws doctrinaire conclusions: the French absolutist state of the seventeenth century, he declares, was above all the instrument by which the dominant economic class continued to exploit the unprivileged. He goes even further, alleging that two powerful forces were in opposition, the popular resistance of the exploited masses and the repressive state organization which sought to stifle it.[78] Such generalizations do scant justice either to the complex judicial framework upon which the state's authority had long been based, or to the intellectual assumptions which dominated men's minds in the mid-seventeenth century. After all, Karl Marx belonged to the nineteenth century, a simple fact which many of his historian disciples, who tend to regard his pronouncements as extra-terrestrial, would do well to remember. Besides, what was this dominant class? Porchnev's inference appears to be that it consisted of those people who ran the state, but there were a great many involved in that operation: does he mean the royal officials, the secretaries of state, the *intendants*, the *élus*, who helped to administer the kingdom, the *traitants* and *partisans* who collected the money, the magistrates at *parlement* and bailiwick level who dispensed the king's justice? Or does he mean the king himself and his family, and the small but extremely wealthy court *élite*; or does he include the whole of the first and second estates which shared so much prestige and so many privileges? And who were the exploited? Were the poor peasants and artisans in the same category as the wealthy *bourgeois,* and what was the position of the provincial estates or the municipal authorities or the assemblies of the clergy which found themselves increasingly hard-pressed by royal agents for even greater economic contributions?

When Porchnev writes about the Fronde itself, the difficulties of defining the opposing forces in his social-economic terms become

[77] R. Mousnier, *Les XVIe et XVIIe siècles* (vol. IV of *Histoire générale des civilisations*), Paris 1961, pp. 161-8.
[78] B. Porchnev. *Les soulèvements populaires en France de 1623 à 1648*, Paris 1963, pp. 293-4.

more apparent. The Fronde began, he alleges, when the *bourgeoisie* provided national leadership for those popular movements which had been causing disruption in one part of the kingdom or another during the first half of the seventeenth century. But who were these middle-class revolutionary leaders?—evidently, in the beginning at least, they were the magistrates of the *parlement* of Paris. In 1648, according to Porchnev, the government required the officers of this court to pay the *paulette*, the annual tax which allowed office-holders to transmit their office to their heirs, for a number of years in advance if they were to retain this privilege. This demand he sees as the abandonment of the *bourgeoisie* by the powers of absolutism, and it resulted in the events of 26 and 27 August 1648 in Paris, when *bourgeois* and proletariat fought side by side at the barricades. In its origins, Porchnev declares, the Fronde was a middle-class revolution in which the nobility played no part whatsoever.[79]

Such an account, however, is at variance with a number of other facts which Porchnev omits to mention and indeed is inaccurate as well as distorted. It is true that certain office-holders, members of the provincial *parlements* and in Paris the members of the *cour des aides*, the *grand conseil* and the *Chambre des comptes* were told that if they wished to retain the right of hereditary transmission of office they had to waive four years' salary. This decision by the government was simply one more disguised financial expedient, savouring of desperation rather than of absolute power. Besides, this policy did not apply to the leaders of revolt, the magistrates of the *parlement* of Paris, the hereditary nature of whose offices was confirmed on 30 April 1648. Certainly in the weeks that followed, the *parlement's* decision to support the other courts and to demand a series of judicial and financial reforms brought that court into particular disfavour in the eyes of the regent, Anne of Austria, and finally persuaded her to have two of its most outspoken members, Broussel and Blancmesnil, arrested. The result of this arrest was dramatic and immediate: the Parisian poor rioted in support of the arrested men, and the Days of the Barricades ensued. There is no evidence that the *parlement* backed this revolt. On the contrary, Broussel's first act after his release was to propose a decree in the *Palais de Justice* ordering the barricades to be pulled down. The fact was that the magistrates alone were in a position to offer a serious and lawful challenge to the government's unpopular policies. In the years since Louis XIII's death, they had opposed a series of financial expedients which had brought hardship to a variety of classes, office-holders, *rentiers*, wealthy middle-class merchants and

---

[79] Porchnev, *Les soulèvements populaires*, p. 521.

also the very poor.[80] They represented no single interest and though they opposed specific government acts they had no wish either to oppose the crown or to side with the *sans-culottes* at the barricades. Nor for that matter did their alliance with the other sovereign court officers last for very long, whilst most members of the wealthy Parisian middle-class took great care to keep themselves entirely apart from the fray.[81] The power of the impact made by the *parlement* of Paris depended upon no such supports nor even upon its attitude to immediate problems and discontents, but upon a tradition of legal independence, upon its ancient duty to speak out in defence of the rights and privileges of all the elements in the state.

The *parlementaire* Fronde ended in April 1649 with the Treaty of Rueil. For Porchnev, this agreement represented a capitulation by the *parlement* and by the *bourgeoisie* in general. In fact the treaty confirmed royal declarations of May, July and October 1648, all of which incorporated government concessions to the magistrates' demands, so that as far as the *parlement* was concerned the Treaty of Rueil was much more a victory than a capitulation. It is worth reiterating, too, that when the agreement was reached the magistrates of the Parisian court were far from being at one with the Parisian middle class. Their relations with the municipal authorities, for example, suggest that the latter were allies from duress as much as from conviction.

Boris Porchnev's marxist interpretation has been severely criticized by Roland Mousnier, in particular in an important article printed in 1958 in the *Revue d'Histoire Moderne et Contemporaine,* entitled '*Recherches sur les soulèvements populaires en France avant la Fronde*'. Mousnier rejects the idea that essentially the revolts grew out of friction between the 'haves' and the 'havenots', the supporters of a feudal monarchy and those whom they exploited. He points out that there was evidence to oppose Porchnev's view that these revolts were almost invariably the spontaneous acts of down-trodden people: on the contrary they were provoked in 1632 by the municipal authorities at Lyons, in 1636 by the *noblesse de race* of Périgord, in 1641 by a prince of the blood, the count of Soissons. In 1643, the conduct of bishops and magistrates in Languedoc was seen by one royal official as likely to encourage sedition there (Doc. 60). From this sort of evidence Mousnier draws his own conclusions about the significance of these outbreaks. The nobility, he believes, was seeking to reverse the process by which the king's officials were extending the crown's authority

[80] Shennan, *The Parlement of Paris*, pp. 255 *et seq.*
[81] A. Lloyd Moote, 'The Parlementary Fronde and Seventeenth-Century Robe solidarity', in *French Historical Studies*, vol. 2 (iii), 1962, pp. 347-52.

at their expense, taxing their peasants to such a degree as to limit the amount that the same peasants could afford to pay in seignorial dues, insinuating the king's justice between themselves and their peasants, reducing their prestige in the local community, trampling upon old rights and privileges. Far from representing the oppressive state, as Porchnev believes, Mousnier asserts that the nobility was itself involved in a struggle against increasing state interference.[82] This aspect of his argument is much more firmly based than his proposition that seventeenth-century office-holders, however distinguished, were not true noblemen but were employed as middle-class agents of the government to support it against the sort of noble-inspired opposition to which he had earlier referred. The dubious nature of this argument is underlined by Mousnier's own subsequent assertion that the monarchy, having stabilized its authority with *bourgeois* assistance, because of grievous financial pressures found itself at odds with the *bourgeoisie* as well, and was forced, in order to retain its position, to rely upon a fresh group of royal agents, new men in his council and in the provinces, the *intendants*.[83] But who were these new men? Were they neither noble nor *bourgeois*? In fact, they had to be one or the other, and they very quickly acquired titles of nobility in return for their services to the king, just as their *bourgeois* predecessors had done. Mousnier's argument seems to suggest that though the king's officers might become the leaders of the *bourgeoisie* they could never aspire to true nobility. Though the clear distinction between *bourgeois* and nobleman remained, the previous history of French government and society amply demonstrates the continuity of movement from one state to the other and refutes Mousnier's statement that the character of the French monarchy changed because of a replacement of the *noblesse d'épee* by the *robins* in the king's council. That distinction was less important than the one between personal and hereditary nobility, though one doubts whether even before 1644, when all the magistrates in the *parlement* of Paris were granted hereditary noble status, Professor Mousnier would have succeeded in convincing many members of that court that they belonged to the *bourgeoisie*. Indeed, it is ironic that the two chief protagonists in this controversy should agree on this, that one of the most important groups in the Fronde, the magistrates of the *parlement*, belonged to the middle class, a judgment at variance with the legal position and insupportable in the general context of that institution's history; it is perhaps even stranger that while the more doctrinaire Russian historian is willing

---

[82] R. Mousnier, 'Recherches sur les soulèvements populaires en France avant la fronde', in *Revue d'histoire moderne et contemporaine*, vol. V, 1958, p. 109.
[83] *Ibid.*, pp. 109-11.

68   GOVERNMENT AND SOCIETY IN FRANCE

to recognize the existence of social aspirations which resulted in an upward movement into the noble class, Professor Mousnier seems not to accept the view, so lucidly argued by his compatriot, Professor J. F. Bluche, that the king did not rely upon middle-class officials since such men, having become royal servants, were invariably and speedily elevated to noble status.[84]

When the marxist approach is broadened to include the whole of Europe it is predictably even more open to criticism. In another well-known contribution to the argument, *The General Crisis of the Seventeenth Century,* Professor Trevor-Roper points out that the marxist case is not proven, that to explain the seventeenth-century revolts both in England and upon the continent of Europe as middle-class movements is one thing, to find the proof is quite another matter. Doctrinaire hypothesis, he maintains, has been substituted for historical evidence and to a non-marxist, at least, his analysis seems irrefutable.[85] Yet his own explanation of the general European crisis appears no less suspect if applied in particular to France. For Trevor-Roper the crisis is to be found in the relations between society and the state. The state of which he writes is the renaissance state, a proliferating bureaucratic machine dominated by the prince, who needed more and more officials to run his councils, staff his tribunals, administer his lands and enforce his authority. The cost of maintaining all these offices fell for the most part not upon the crown but upon the country; indeed, the crown was pleased to sell offices at an ever higher cost as a means of obtaining valuable funds. The growing financial burden of the state, therefore, with its mass of profiteering office-holders, is for Trevor-Roper the universal irritant which provoked revolution. Those who revolted were those who suffered most from the weight of taxation: the gentry in England, the peasantry in France.[86]

This interpretation, so plausible and attractive in general terms, loses much of its appeal when applied to a particular area. As with Porchnev the problem of definition becomes paramount: what constituted the state and who represented the country, was this a straightforward clash between the wealthy and the impoverished? In the case of France, Professor Mousnier has clearly underlined the contradictions of the theory. Although there were many complaints levelled against office-holders and their revenue in seventeenth-century France, Mousnier points out that there were

[84] J. F. Bluche, 'L'origine sociale des secrétaires d'état de Louis XIV (1661-1715),' in *Le dix-septième siècle,* vols XLII-XLIII, 1959, p. 22.
[85] Trevor-Roper, 'The General Crisis of the Seventeenth Century', pp. 35-7.
[86] Trevor-Roper, 'The General Crisis of the Seventeenth Century', pp. 42 *et seq.*

just as many complaints about the difficulty and expense of purchasing office (Doc. 70).[87] In other words, the protagonists were not so tidily divided into opposing camps as Trevor-Roper would have us believe. Indeed, in his terms the situation becomes extremely confusing. What was the position of the magistrates of the *parlement* of Paris during the Fronde? Did they represent the oppressed country, those elements in society which for too long had paid for the financial benefits enjoyed by the office-holders? Hardly, since they were themselves among the nation's leading office-holders. They ought surely to have been on the side of the state machine, the object not the instigators of revolt. How was it then that they found themselves in opposition to the very embodiment of the state, the king himself?

Perhaps enough has now been said to indicate that in the particular case of France current historical ideas about a mid-century crisis lead in mutually exclusive directions. That being so, it becomes impossible to support the theory of a general European crisis, since France cannot be included in any all-embracing interpretation until a measure of agreement about the French situation is reached, and to talk of a general European crisis without France would be nonsense. But what of the position of France alone? Has the hallucinatory vision of a general crisis lured historians into contemplating an equally fictitious particular one? The contradictory conclusions outlined above seem to suggest so, at least in so far as historians have envisaged a fundamentally revolutionary situation. It cannot be denied, of course, that the country suffered a series of widespread revolts in the seventeenth century culminating in the civil wars of the Fronde when the king was forced to leave his own capital, and such a state of affairs undoubtedly posed serious political problems. But a distinction must be made between a crisis reflecting a grave undermining of the established order and a situation which almost resolved itself, whilst the king was still a minor, his regent a woman and his chief minister the most hated man in France. The first half of the seventeenth century has become a source of myopic attraction to historians and they have drawn sharper contours around those years than are justified on any long-term view.

Professor Robert Mandrou has helped to put the seventeenth-century French situation into a broader perspective, and as a result of his observations that period loses a good deal of its recently acquired significance. He draws attention, for example, to the fact that popular revolts were traditional in France, that most of them began as protests against fiscal demands which were intolerable to

[87] Mousnier, 'Discussion of H. R. Trevor-Roper: The General Crisis of the Seventeenth Century', p. 10.

people already suffering grievous economic hardship. He emphasizes that short-term considerations were responsible for the most part— a new tax, a new tax-collector, a new system of tax-collecting, and that almost always the movements fizzled out very quickly (Doc. 71). Even more important was the fact that there were few signs of a genuinely revolutionary attitude. On the contrary, there were positive signs of continuing loyalty to the monarchical principle as some of the rebels' slogans indicate: 'Vive le roi sans la gabelle' and 'Vive le roi sans la taille'. Nor was that other bastion of the French establishment, the Church, ever threatened; the tenth, which was a substantial tax, was invariably paid without a murmur.[88] The Fronde, of course, cannot be dismissed quite so easily. It was a compound of various elements, chiefly economic hardship and dissatisfaction in a number of quarters with the government's extension and abuse of its traditional powers, exacerbated by the abnormal condition of a regency and the highly personal animosity directed against Cardinal Mazarin. These cumulative tensions finally produced the outbreak. It failed, however, because none of the elements of opposition were capable, or even desirous, of raising their antagonism to a revolutionary level. The Fronde was a far less serious threat to the established order than the Wars of Religion had been; it was one of a number of points at which the requirements of the central government—especially in the financial field—clashed with the customary doctrines of the subjects' rights and privileges, guaranteed by the law. This was already a well-established source of tension in 1648 and it would persist in the future far beyond that date. For some time to come, however, the power and prestige of the crown would remain a sufficient guarantee for the continuity of the French political tradition.

CONCLUSION

The interest in mid-seventeenth century French history recently aroused amongst historians justifies a full discussion of the issues raised and the solutions proposed. Such a discussion is doubly valuable, however, for the events of the Fronde in particular highlight some of the chief factors affecting the development of French government and society which were permanently significant, though usually less spectacularly demonstrated. Chief amongst them was respect for the crown, which more than any other single factor gave the State stability and identity. Of course the actual power of the king varied according to changing situations and personalities, but

[88] R. Mandrou, *Classes et luttes de classes en France au début du XVIIe siècle*, Florence 1965, pp. 64-76.

the important thing was that the crown's position in the structure of politics and in the political theory of government did not alter. Even though an individual ruler or a group of his subjects might abuse that position, the fundamental and paradoxical balance of unlimited authority and the supremacy of the law was only ever temporarily compromised.

The whole of the period is characterized by this strong element of continuity, but inevitably there was change too. It would be foolish indeed to imagine that these two hundred years were static, almost petrified in terms of political development. Yet it was the peculiar nature of the French state that though tensions were constantly being created they were contained within the existing framework. The chief cause of tension—again the Fronde offers the best illustration—was the gradually increasing role of the central government which threatened to trample over the ancient rights and privileges which were a part of the French inheritance. In this matter, the king acted pragmatically on occasion, seeking to provide for the needs of his state as best he could in the circumstances but not seeking to reform the political structure in order to achieve better results. In other words, there is little virtue in seeing the development of fifteenth-to-seventeenth-century France in terms of the growth of absolute monarchy. Despite occasions when the crown or its opponents exceeded the generally accepted norm, that norm remained the standard subsequently to be reasserted. Thus the direction of the *régime* was less progressive than cyclical. This is particularly apparent in the sphere of social mobility. It is not the case that the king's new men were steadily advancing his authority at the expense of a discredited class; on the contrary, the new men were being continually absorbed into the establishment, moving up as those whom they were replacing had done before them, into the higher reaches of the first and second estates. Though the towns were gradually brought under closer royal control, their leading officers were still able to move from *bourgeois* to noble status. All the important crown offices, old and new, continued to wield judicial as well as administrative powers, and none of them, the bailiff, the lieutenant-general, the treasurer, the *élu* or the *intendant,* possessed a new kind of authority which set him apart from the rest, though each of them was at a different level on the social ladder. There were jurisdictional disputes between them and allegations levelled against the newer officials that they were guilty not only of trespassing upon the preserves of established authorities, but also of ignoring the legal rules by which the government's affairs should have been conducted. The *intendants* in particular came in for this sort of criticism, and once more the Fronde clearly illustrates how the existence of different groups of royal officials gave rise to mutual jealousy and antagonism.

These stresses were a reflection of the more generalized tension generated by the limitations upon royal authority. There was no system for the sovereign to regulate. His office represented the state, and he acted as he saw fit when the need for action arose. He saw nothing unusual or contradictory in nominating officials to carry out the same tasks as other previously appointed men. Nothing could be more misleading than to interpret French monarchical government as simply a less sophisticated version of the twentieth-century system; it was fundamentally different in character. Yet precisely because there was no system, the need to preserve normal judicial procedures was considered most important, and the king had to balance this requirement against his undoubted right to establish and give authority to whatever new offices he wished. In this matter, too, the tension remained, though particular conflicts were normally resolved without a serious situation being provoked.

Long before the end of this period most offices had become venal and hereditary. The king needed money, and the sale of office was an effective way of acquiring it. It is easy enough to argue that such a method was inefficient and fraught with danger for the monarchy; but inefficiency implies the misuse of a kind of machinery which no French king either possessed or envisaged. As for the danger, it is true that the sale of office encumbered the government with some inadequate officials, some unimpressive family dynasties, though it seems unlikely that any other method of selection conceivable at the time would have ensured the emergence of men of higher calibre. In addition these office-holders formed an ever-increasing group of creditors, permanently embarrassing the crown which had been grateful for their money in the first instance but had then to find the annual interest payments in return. However, there is another side to the coin. Had it not been for the practice of venality, the degree of mobility within the existing framework, which effectively prevented any dangerous hardening of the social arteries, would have been more difficult to achieve and the possibility of serious friction would have been that much greater. Nor should the financial value of offices be given too much prominence. Honours and dignities were more important in French society than mere wealth, a fact demonstrated by the frequency of royal acts forbidding the nobility to make money. Most French magistrates, for example, unlike many of their English counterparts, were far more concerned with the social status of their offices than with their financial possibilities. There is one more point to be made about venal and hereditary office-holding. Though some royal officials were inadequate, they did at least possess a degree of freedom from royal interference. In a state where all decisions ultimately assumed a judicial character, where the king's power was unlimited save by the law, there were good reasons why the judges should be independent. A number of seventeenth-century Englishmen would certainly have appreciated the point.

In conclusion, the picture of French government and society which emerges from the period 1461–1661 is one of fundamental stability founded on the role of the monarchy, a stability which survived—though only just during the Wars of Religion—a variety of internal pressures. However, stability and continuity must not be mistaken for rigidity. There was constant tension, constant pressure and counter-pressure, poise and equipoise, between the crown and the various component parts of the state, as each sought to adjust to changes without invoking a revolution. That this tension was for the most part contained depended in political terms upon the absence of a written constitution and of any desire to categorize the traditionally accepted rights and limitations of monarch and subject; and in social terms upon the absence of rigid barriers which could thwart ambitious men and lead them eventually to challenge the monarchy itself.

DOCUMENTS

A. Power and its Limitations

(i). The Monarchy

I (a). FROM CLAUDE DE SEYSSEL, *La Monarchie de France*, ed.
J. Poujol, Paris, 1961, pp. 113–119.

The authority and power of the king in France is regulated and
restrained by three checks ... the first is Religion, the second, Justice
and the third, Police. ...

With regard to the first, it is an indisputable fact that the French
have always been, and still are ... pious and god-fearing. .. For that
reason it is both proper and necessary that whoever is king should
make it known to the people by example and by visible and outward
signs that he is a zealot, an observer of the Faith and of the
Christian religion, and that he is resolved to use his power to
sustain and strengthen it ... so long as the king respects ... the
Christian religion he cannot act as a tyrant. If he is guilty of such
an act, it is permissible for a prelate or any other devout man of
religion who respects the people, to remonstrate with and to up-
braid him, and for a simple preacher to rebuke and accuse him
publicly as well as in private. ...

Justice, which is the second check ... indubitably carries more
weight in France than in any other country in the world, especially
because of the institution of the *Parlements,* whose principal role is
to bridle the absolute power which kings might seek to use... In the
matter of distributive justice the king has always been subject to
these courts, so that in civil cases an individual may gain satisfaction and justice indiscriminately against the king or against his subjects. As far as criminal cases are concerned, royal pardons and
remissions are so contested, and those who obtain them are the
subject of such violent argument that, lacking hope and confidence
in such remissions, few people dare to act in an ill-advised, much
less in a thoroughly odious manner. ... Besides, justice is that much
more powerful because those who are deputed to administer it have
permanent possession of their offices and the king has no power to
remove them, save in the event of forfeiture. ...

The third check is that of Police, by which is intended those many
ordinances that have been promulgated, and subsequently confirmed
and approved from time to time, by the kings themselves, which

help to preserve the kingdom as a whole and the rights of the individuals who compose it.

1 (b). FROM IBID., p. 130.

Regarding the monarchical state, since everything depends upon the monarch it appears that no other remedy for abuse is required, no other means of maintaining order is necessary than that the king should be good. Because he commands the entire obedience of his subjects he can, without difficulty, enforce the observance and maintenance of good laws, ordinances and customs, he can correct and annul those which are not beneficial or completely faultless, and he can make new laws if necessary; by living in a law-abiding way himself he can induce his subjects to follow his example and ... do what is right....

1 (c). FROM M. DE L'HÔPITAL, *Oeuvres inédites*, ed. J. Dufey, 2 vols, Paris, 1825, vol. 1, part IV, pp. 380–81, *Traité de la Réformation de la Justice*.

It is loyal advice to French princes to treat their subjects with such moderation, mildness and benevolence and principally with such justice and lawfulness as to enable their subjects to perceive thereby that their affection is more paternal than lordly, more temperate than absolute, more venerable than terrible or awe-inspiring and that they hold as enemies and wicked men those who would counsel them differently. I have no wish, however, to approve rebellion against the monarch, however difficult, unjust or extortionate he may be, for I am aware that the subject, like a child, never has a just cause for revolting against his sovereign. Yet the wise man's advice that fathers should not provoke their children to anger by harsh, ill-natured treatment may be applied equally to all who have management or authority over people, even to sovereign princes who are, or ought to be, the fathers of their country.

1 (d). FROM C. LOYSEAU, *Cinq Livres du Droit des Offices avec le Livre des Seigneuries et celui des Ordres*, Paris, 1614, *Traité des Seigneuries*, chapter II, p. 15.

Sovereignty consists in absolute power, that is to say in full and complete authority in every respect, what canon lawyers call the plenitude of power, and is consequently without superior, since he who has a superior cannot be supreme and sovereign. There can be no limitation in time since that would imply neither absolute power nor even lordship but only power held in custody or on trust. Nor can there be any exception of persons or of things appertaining to the state, for such exceptions would automatically cease to belong to it. Just as the crown's circle must be complete if it is to be truly a crown, so too true sovereignty must be entire.

However, since only God is all-powerful, the authority of men can never be entirely absolute: there are three kinds of law which limit the sovereign's power without affecting his sovereignty. These are the laws of God, for the prince's sovereignty is not diminished by his subjection to God; the natural, not positive rules of justice, since ... one attribute of sovereignty is that it should be exercised according to the precepts of justice and not arbitrarily; and finally the fundamental laws of the state, because the prince must exert his sovereignty in the correct way, adhering both to the form and to the conditions which governed that sovereignty from the beginning.

2. FROM T. & D. GODEFROY, *Le Cérémonial Français*, Paris, 1649, vol. I, p. 257, Coronation Oath of Francis I.

To the Prelates: I promise and give you my word that I will scrupulously uphold the canonical privileges, due authority and jurisdiction belonging to each of you and to the churches in your keeping, that I will defend and protect you, with God's help, to the best of my ability, according to the obligation which the king owes to every bishop and church in his kingdom.

To the People: In the name of Jesus Christ, I promise the following to the Christian people subject to me: first, that through our authority all Christian people will always maintain true peace in the Church of God. Item, that I will forbid all individuals, of whatever sort or condition, to indulge in rapacity and injustice. Item, that I will command and ordain that all judgments must be based on standards of equity and clemency so that a merciful and compassionate God may bestow his clemency upon me and upon you. Item, that it is my sincere intention to employ all the authority and power at my disposal to annihilate and drive out from the land subject to my jurisdiction, all heretics pointed out and denounced by the Church. All these things I vow and affirm to observe and accomplish.

3 (a). FROM M. DE L'HÔPITAL, *Oeuvres Inédites*, vol. I, part III, pp. 205–206, *Traité de la Réformation de la Justice.*

There is nothing more just or necessary ... than to obey the orders and wishes of the sovereign prince; that is certainly the case when they are based on justice and good sense. Equity is the nerve, indeed the soul of the law and when it is present that law must receive pure and simple obedience; otherwise, the bond uniting civil society would be broken, there would no longer be any difference between king and subject, and that would create a fine confusion, to prevent which it is very reasonable that the king and his justice should compel obedience. But when the law is prejudicial to the public is it not true that it will recoil upon the prince himself? As chief of state, he is so intimately united with his subjects that he cannot offend nor injure them without himself feeling the effect sooner or later. As the prince is only human it is possible for him to be deceived either inadvertently or by evil and insidious counsel; with more reliable information he will change his mind and in this case a refusal to obey, so far from being imputed to disobedience and disservice, should be seen as one of the greatest and most notable services that can be done for him, for probably his intention is not to wrong or injure his people but rather to procure for them well-being and prosperity, indeed to put his own personal profit after that of his subjects. ...

3 (b). FROM OMER TALON, *Mémoires, continués par Denis Talon* (vol. XXX of *Nouvelle Collection des Mémoires*, ed. J. F. Michaud and J. J. F. Poujoulat, 34 vols, Paris 1854).

And in fact, Francis I ... having complained in this place of the difficulties made in registering certain edicts which ordered the creation of new offices, did not cause the letters to be published in his presence because he knew well that verification consists in liberty of suffrage, and that it is a kind of illusion in morals and a contradiction in politics to believe that edicts which by the laws of the kingdom are not susceptible of execution until they have been brought to the sovereign companies and there debated, shall pass for verified when Your Majesty has had them read and published in his presence. And so all who have occupied our places, those great personages who have preceded us, whose memory will always be honourable because they defended courageously the rights of the king their master and the interests of the public, which are inseparable, have on like occasions cried out with much more vigour than we could possibly do; the *parlement* has made remonstrances full of affection and fidelity.

... You are, Sire, our sovereign Lord; the power of Your Majesty comes from above, who owe an account of your actions, after God, only to your conscience; but it concerns your glory that we be free men and not slaves; the grandeur of your state and the dignity of your crown are measured by the quality of those who obey you.

3 (c). FROM IBID., p. 268.

Formerly the king's wishes were never executed by his subjects without being first approved by all the great men of the kingdom, by the princes and officers of the crown; today this political jurisdiction is vested in the *Parlement*; our possession of this power is guaranteed by a long tradition and respectfully acknowledged by the people. The opposition of our votes, the respectful resistance which we bring to bear in public affairs must not be interpreted as disobedience but rather as a necessary result of the exercise of our office and of the fulfilling of our obligations, and certainly the king's majesty is not diminished by his having to respect the decrees of his kingdom; by so doing, he governs, in the words of the Scriptures, a lawful kingdom.

4 (a). FROM J. BODIN, *The Six Bookes of a Commonweale*, ed. K. D. McRae, (a facsimile reprint of the English translation of 1606, Harvard Political Classics), Cambridge, Mass., 1962, Book 3, chapter 1, p. 267.

Wherewith the king (Charles IX) displeased, caused his privie Counsell to be called, and by the authoritie thereof a decree to bee made the xxiiii of September, whereby the Parlament [sic] of Paris was forbidden once to call in question the lawes or decrees proceeding from the king concerning matters of state: which was also before by king Francis decreed in the yeare 1528.

4 (b). FROM P. R. DOOLIN, *The Fronde*, Harvard U.P., 1935, pp. 79–80, Royal Declaration, July 31, 1652.

... All authority ... belongs to us. We hold it of God alone, and no person, of whatever quality he may be, can pretend to any part of it. ... The functions of justice, of arms, of finance, should be always distinct and separate; the officers of the Parlement have no other power than that which we have deigned to entrust to them, to render justice to our subjects. They have no more right to regulate ... and take cognizance of what is not of their jurisdictions, than the officers of our armies and our finances would have to render justice, or establish presidents and counsellors to exercise it. ... Will posterity ever believe

F

that officers have presumed to preside over the general government of the Kingdom, form councils and collect taxes, to assume, finally, the plenitude of a power which belongs only to us?

4 (c). FROM IBID., pp. 135–6, *Lettre d'avis à messieurs du Parlement de Paris,* anon., Paris, 1649.

... When the Kings come to the crown, they swear on the holy Gospels that they will maintain the Church of God to their best ability; that they will observe the fundamental laws of the State, and that they will protect their subjects according to God and reason, as good Kings should do; and in consideration of this oath, the people are obligated to obey them as Gods on earth; and the oath to do so which they swore to the first Kings still endures, because of the perpetual succession which is maintained in France. Both oaths are respective; and just as the King can cause subjects to be punished severely who have broken the promise which they have made to obey him as their legitimate Monarch, in all matters not contrary to the three fundamental articles which I have stated; so subjects are exempt from obedience, when Kings violate their oath; for if they overturn the laws of the Church, who is the subject who will obey them, and who is obligated to obey them? That is the great question, in fact, of the time of Henry IV, to which he could find a solution only by making himself a Catholic. If they break the fundamental laws of the State, if, for example, they pretend to cause the Kingdom to fall to the distaff, to sell or alienate their domain, the subjects are not bound to give them another, or to obey them on the other point. All this is without difficulty; and one must conclude that it is the same for the third circumstance of the oath, that if the Kings do not protect their subjects according to right and reason, in conformity with the laws of God and the Ordinances of the Estates which the sovereign Courts are bound to cause to be executed, having them in trust, the subjects are exempt from obedience; and even more, if they are oppressed unjustly, and with tyrannical violence, which cannot be reconciled with Royal Monarchy, in which the subjects obligate themselves to the Kings only to be protected against those who might trouble their repose; so that, if they trouble it themselves, they cease to be Kings, and the subjects to be subjects.

5. FROM P. R. DOOLIN, *The Fronde,* p. 94.
FROM anon. pamphlet, *Response Chrestienne et Politique aux Opinions Erronées du Temps,* 1652.

It is true that the King is obliged, and promises at his Consecration, to render Justice, and to govern his Kingdom according to right and reason; when he does not keep his promise God, who is sole Judge of his actions, will not leave his injustice unpunished, but it does not belong to subjects to take cognizance of them, nor to judge if his commands are just and reasonable, for if it were permissible everyone would be King above the King, since he would have power not only to control what he did, but also to take all that seemed to him reasonable, and to reject everything that he did not approve. The Kings, to show their sovereign power and to indicate that they are obliged to render an account of their actions to God alone, use these words, *Car tel est nostre plaisir*, as the Sovereign Courts say in their decrees ... to show their sovereignty.

6 (a). FROM *Actions et Traités Oratoires de Guillaume du Vair*, ed. R. Radouant, Paris, 1911, pp. 214–21, *Harangue of the first president of the Parlement of Paris, Achille de Harlay*, 1586.

We have two kinds of law, Sire; first there are the laws and ordinances made by kings, secondly there are the ordinances of the kingdom, immutable and inviolable, according to which you yourself have acquired this royal throne and crown, handed down to you in succession from your predecessors. God has put great power in your hands, Sire, and you could, if you wished, do with us and with our possessions whatever you pleased, but it is not God's intention that you should ever contemplate ruling by violence and force. Such reigns are those of pirates and robbers and as such their aspect and condition changes with each season of the year. But your reign is one of probity and justice and your subjects render you more submission and obedience willingly than the Turks and Barbarians give to their princes as a result of force and compulsion. Why should this be so? It is, Sire, because the law of the country in which they are born, the law which governs them, obliges them chiefly to love the king after God, and to live only for him.

6 (b). FROM IBID., p. 99, Guillaume du Vair, *Exhortation in Favour of Peace*, 1593.

I declare, therefore, that as far as human judgment can comprehend the matter, not one of the suggestions so far made can offer a remedy for our troubles, and give peace to this poor and desolate kingdom and security for our religion.

Only one possibility remains, to convert the king of Navarre to catholicism and make him king of France. He is the premier prince, and the crown belongs to him by right of birth. If he were a catholic, nobody would have any objection.

7 (a). FROM T. & D. GODEFROY, *Le Cérémonial Français*, vol. I, p. 77, Jean Jouvenal des Ursins (1388–1473), Archbishop of Rheims to Louis XI, whom he consecrated in 1461.

At his consecration the king of France becomes an ecclesiastical figure ... [to Charles VII]. As far as you are concerned, my sovereign lord, you are not simply a layman but a spiritual personage, a prelate.... And as the head and chief ecclesiastical figure [of the French Church] you can call together your prelates and with them princes of the royal blood... should anyone wish to dispute it I will stand up and relate how in the year 1398 the matter was boldly discussed and it was agreed that you may preside over the council of your church of France, that after receiving the advice of the church, of the princes of the blood and of your council, you may pass judgment on the liberties and freedoms of your church and erect them into a law, an ordinance, a pragmatic sanction, and you may take all due and proper measures to see that the law is kept and observed.

7 (b). FROM M. BLOCH, *Les Rois Thaumaturges*, Paris, 1924, p. 482, Extracts from the *Traité du Sacre* of Jean Golein written in 1372, printed in 1503.

... those who are infected with scrofula are soon cured and restored to health if they are touched by the king's hand, after his anointing from the holy phial....

7 (c). FROM IBID., pp. 487–88.

... No woman has ever been consecrated with royal unction, a ceremony which brings the recipient close to the priestly state, nor has a woman ever been entrusted with the role of curing scrofula by touch. It is evident from these facts that women neither can nor ought to inherit the French kingdom... neither by succession nor by election ... the kingdom of France is held together by the succession of the nearest male heir in the royal line.

7 (d). FROM IBID., p. 362.

Be it known to all concerned that on next Sunday, Easter day, his Majesty will touch those afflicted with scrofula, at ten o'clock in the morning in the galleries of the Louvre....

Issued at Paris, in the king's presence, on March 26th, 1657.
Signed: de Souches.

8 (a). FROM Recueil générale des Anciennes Lois Françaises, Paris,
1822–33, ed. F. Isambert, vol. XII, pp. 79 *et seq, The Concordat
of Bologna, Concerning Elections, Rubric I.*

With the advice and unanimous approval of our brothers, with our
certain knowledge and full authority, we hereby enact and ordain that
henceforth and forever in the future in place of the pragmatic sanction
or constitution and of each and every chapter contained therein, the
following shall be observed:
Henceforward, in the case of vacancies now and in the future in
cathedral and metropolitan churches of the said kingdom [of France]
... provided that such vacancies have been voluntarily assigned to us
and to our successors canonically appointed bishops of Rome, the
chapters and monks of these churches may not proceed to the election
or postulation of the future prelate. In the event of such a vacancy
whoever is king of France shall within six months counting from the
day on which the vacancy occurred present and nominate to us and
to our successors, as bishops of Rome or to the apostolic see to be
invested by us, a sober or knowledgeable master or graduate in
theology, or a doctor or graduate in all or in one of the laws taught and
rigorously examined at a famous university, who must be at least twenty-
seven years old and otherwise suitable ... and should the king not nominate a person with such qualifications, neither we, nor our successors
nor the Holy See shall have to invest such a person ... and as regards
monasteries and conventual priories ... in the case of present and
future vacancies, provided that they have been assigned in a similar
fashion [to those above-mentioned] the monasteries may not henceforth proceed to the election or postulation of abbots or priors; when
a vacancy occurs, the king ... must make the nomination and the
person thus nominated to the vacant monastery will be invested by us
and by our successors. And the priories will be similarly conferred
upon persons nominated by the king. If, within the stipulated six
months, the king should present to us, our successors or the Holy See
a secular priest or a regular priest of another order or a minor under
twenty-three years or someone unsuitable in another way, such a person
will be rejected by us and will not be invested with the office. Within
three months of the date of our rejection the king will have to nominate
another candidate with the above-mentioned qualifications. And the
person thus nominated will be invested with the title to the vacant
monastery by us, our successors or the Holy See. The office of prior
will be conferred similarly upon properly qualified candidates....

Given at Rome at a public assembly held in the holy consecrated church of the Lateran, in the year of Our Lord 1516, the 14 day of January and the fourth year of our Pontificate. . . .

Wherefore our dear and well-beloved councillors at present and in the future members of our *parlements* and all judges in our kingdom . . . and other officers and subjects are commanded and charged, to the extent that each is involved, closely to maintain, respect and observe all the above-mentioned decisions. . . .

Given at Paris, on the 13 day of May, in the year of Our Lord 1517, in the third year of our reign.

8 (b). FROM IBID., p. 98, *Papal Bull on the Annates (De Annatis)*, *October, 1516.* Bishop Leo, the servant of the servants of God. . . .

In the concordat which we have concluded with our dear son in Jesus Christ, Francis, king of France, for the glory of God and for the peace and tranquillity of Christians, and with the advice of our brothers, we ruled that the provision of vacant benefices accorded by us and our successors or by the Holy See to subjects of the kingdom of France . . . even to persons nominated to cathedral and metropolitan churches and to monasteries should only be maintained if the annual value of the benefices was declared in the form of golden ducats from the apostolic chamber, *livres tournois* or another currency; otherwise these favours would be nullified.

9. FROM *Lettres de Henri III, Roi de France,* ed. M. François, Paris, 1965, vol. II, pp. 85–6, 1178. To Pope Gregory XIII, Avignon, December 26, 1574.

Most Holy Father. It has pleased God to call to Himself our most dear and well-beloved cousin, Charles, Cardinal of Lorraine. We are filled with feelings of the deepest grief because of this great loss to the Holy Apostolic See, to whose service he was entirely devoted. . . . We have given our *lettres de placet* to Your Holiness in favour of our cousin Loys of Lorraine, his nephew, the son of our late cousin the *duc de* Guise who was killed at Orléans, in order that he may be invested with the majority of the benefices which he [the late Cardinal] possessed in our kingdom, including the Archbishopric of Rheims, as you will see from the despatches which will be presented to you; besides which we have desired to write to Your Holiness to beg him, which we do as affectionately as we can, both for love of us and in contemplation of the services which our late cousin the Cardinal of

Lorraine, his uncle and all his relatives have performed for the Holy Apostolic See, to see fit to confer on our cousin, Loys of Lorraine, the vacant see and the annates appertaining to the archbishopric and to other benefices; and seeing that our most dear and well-beloved cousin the cardinal de Guise, the brother of the dead man, has not yet any priestly title, may it please Your Holiness to grant him the title of Saint Apolinaire which belonged to our late cousin, Charles, the Cardinal of Lorraine, and likewise to grant him too the legateship of Lorraine with the same rights as his brother, our late cousin, the Cardinal of Lorraine, in addition conceding to him a mandate to proceed in the matter of the alienation of church property in this kingdom accorded to us, in the place of our late cousin, his brother; together with another mandate to empower him to consecrate and crown us at Rheims. . . .

10. FROM IBID., vol. II, pp. 30–1, 1057. To the *seigneur de* Ferrals (beginning of October 1574, Lyons).

Monsieur de Ferrailz [sic], on a number of occasions I have asked our Holy Father's nuncio to produce the bull that His Holiness has been willing to grant for the transfer and sale of church property so that it may be sent to the members of my court of *parlement* in Paris; there it can be published and registered, a customary and necessary procedure as you know for the security of the purchasers. However, the nuncio has failed to deliver it, alleging that he has not received orders to do so from His Holiness. . . . I have spoken to him about it myself and so has the Queen, my mother, who has taken the trouble to point out to him more particularly the extent to which this state of affairs hindered and prejudiced my affairs, seeing that my current expenses for the maintenance of my armies and foreign troops are assigned to the revenue which ought to result from the above mentioned sale, a large proportion of which is already spent and owing. [She has also pointed out] that nobody will come forward to buy this property until the bull has been confirmed by my courts of *parlement* which cannot act until they have received the original copy of the bull which I do not consider our Holy Father granted and despatched in order that it should remain useless and ineffective in the hands of his nuncio. I have caused my cousin, the Cardinal of Lorraine, to say as much to him. . . . I beg you to speak [to His Holiness] immediately you receive this letter so that he may write at once to his nuncio with orders to hand over the bull without further difficulty and delay since I must have it if His Holiness wants me to receive help from it in time.

11. FROM RENÉ DE LUCINGE, SIRE OF LES ALLYMES, *Dialogue du François et du Savoysien* (1593), ed. A. Dufour, Paris, 1963, pp. 241 *et seq.*

The Savoyard: The meeting of these Estates will not be of great service to France because you have no desire to have a foreigner as king and you have no native candidate; since you are in this state of irresolution and the problem of religion is causing you such scruples, you will require lengthy deliberations before procuring the results which you hope for in your affairs; in short, according to your reckoning, you are taking a risk whether you elect a king or approve the accession of the king of Navarre.

The Frenchman: I have told you that the Pope and the king of Spain have wished us to assemble in this fashion. I believe that the Pope has the interest of the church in mind and the king of Spain his own interest, for he will either divide us if we trust him or he will leave us an enfeebled prey to our enemies; he fears too that our princes are not very happy about their present situation, that they are not satisfied with their sway [gouvernement] and might make a damaging arrangement with the king of Navarre, recognizing him in return for being allowed to live as they wish. This king, who for his part, is tired of so many wars, who needs to advance and make progress, in whatever fashion he receives his so-called subjects, will by this means restore his fortunes, recover his breath, gain reinforcements and thus become, quite peaceably, the master of his subjects and of their religion. ... I do not doubt that this long truce will lead to a settlement. If that happens it will leave a thorn in the Spaniard's foot; whilst if we elect a king we shall find ourselves even more fiercely engaged in war. The elected ruler will necessarily depend on Spain whence he will have received favours and will normally continue to receive them in order to maintain his position. He will lean upon her and embark on a fierce war against his rival: that is the object at which Spain is aiming and thus we would find ourselves in a more bloody war than ever.

The Savoyard: If the king of Navarre became a catholic, if, as you say, he satisfied the princes, would this give you some shadow of that peace which you have been so uncertainly seeking in your affairs?

The Frenchman: This word peace, quiet, tranquillity, conveys a thousand and one comforts in itself. I strongly believe that whilst we only concern ourselves with individual human problems saying nothing about the faith, then it is easy to achieve peace; but that would be to make peace with men and not with God. Our religion would still be very insecure for some time after his [Henry of Navarre's] conversion. Who can be certain of his greatness of soul? And, even if he promises, would he be willing to keep faith later? Finally, the Pope would have to approve of him for this scruple would hold back a number of our Frenchmen in the united party [the League] who would rather be torn apart than acknowledge him otherwise.

The Savoyard: And yet would it not be better to unite the two parties and thus impel this king, who ought to be the successor to your crown, to become a catholic, rather than follow the vain hopes and fancies of an election? His intentions will be clear in a few months, and if he wishes to deceive God or plots in his heart against our religion doubtless there will be a speedy recourse to arms and he will not prosper. As for the Pope's approval, I estimate—if I dare meddle in such weighty matters—that it is better for him to save our religion from the great peril of being banished from the whole of France by the force of this king's arms, than to provoke him; almost certainly it is better to receive him than to risk this limb of the Church, which is already on the point of seceding from its obedience to Rome. For if he [Henry] asks to be received into the Church it will be on conditions which will testify to his conversion and which will guarantee our trust; in that case His Holiness terminates a great peril, arrests the progress of a great danger. . . .

The Frenchman: It is always a case of postponing matters to allow us to see what we must come to, but we should like to capitulate positively, if possible, and not conditionally.

The Savoyard: You will soon reach the most convenient agreement as a result of this conversion to catholicism and you will welcome it to thwart the designs of Spain.

12. FROM P. PITHOU, *Les Libertés de l'Eglise Gallicane*, 5 vols, Lyons, 1771, vols I–II, Articles I–LXVI, *passim.*

The details of these liberties might seem infinite, yet serious consideration will reveal that they all depend on two closely connected maxims, which France has always held to be indisputable. . . . The first is that Popes cannot command nor ordain anything in general or in specific matters appertaining to the temporal affairs of the lands and country under the obedience and sovereignty of the most christian king; and if they should so command or decree, the king's subjects, even including clerics, do not have to obey. . . . The second is that although the Pope is recognized as suzerain in spiritual matters yet in France there is no place for absolute and limitless power and [his authority] is curbed and confined by those canons and regulations of the ancient councils of the Church which have been received in this kingdom. *Et in hoc maxime consistit libertas Ecclesiae Gallicanae*; with these appropriate words, the University of Paris (which is the defender . . . of the key of our christianity and which has always been a very solicitous promoter and guardian of these rights) argued its case at a plenary session of the *parlement* when it was opposing the verification of bulls concerning the legation of Cardinal d'Amboise. Upon those two maxims depend, either conjointly or separately, a number of other particular ones which have been more practised and executed than written about by our ancestors, according to the occurences and situations which have presented themselves. . . . The most christian king, duly anointed, the eldest son and protector of the catholic church, when he sends his ambassadors to a newly elected Pope to congratulate him on his elevation and to acknowledge him as spiritual father and head of the church militant, has not been accustomed to use expressions of such exact obedience as a number of other princes do, who have some special duty or particular obligation towards the Holy See of Rome, as vassals, tributaries, or in some other capacity: but he only recommends himself and the kingdom over which God has given him sovereignty, together with the Gallican Church, to the favours of His Holiness. . . . The Pope cannot dispose of the kingdom of France and its dependencies as a prize or give it away, nor may he deprive the king or dispose of it in any other way whatsoever. And whatever monitions, excommunications or interdictions he may pronounce, the subjects must not cease to render to the king the obedience which is due to the temporal power, a duty from which they cannot be dispensed nor absolved by the Pope. . . Nor can the king's officers be excommunicated in the exercise of their commissions and offices: and if that should happen, whoever is responsible for the proceedings will be compelled by penalities and fines and by the seizure of his temporalty if he be a cleric, to have such censures revoked. Nor are these officers deemed to be included in the terms of the general monitions in so far as their duties are concerned. . . . Bulls or apostolic letters of summons, executory, fulminary or otherwise, may not have effect in France without letters of approval (*pareatis*) from the king or his officers: and their subsequent execution by the secular courts after permission has been granted will be in the hands of an ordinary royal judge acting with the king's authority and not *auctoritate Apostolica*, in order to avoid confusion and an intermingling of jurisdictions. . . . The right that is known as *régale,* supported by many holy decrees, seems capable of being fitted into the liberties of the Gallican Church since it depends upon the first of the general maxims enunciated above. For although many great personages have distinguished two sorts or kinds of *régale,* temporal and spiritual, a close examination will reveal that both flow from a single source, or one might say, a single right, not, indeed, one of redemption or relief, but rather the right to lease, guard, protect. . . . Also, the *régale* is pre-eminent in that . . . it is subject only to the jurisdiction and cognizance of the king and his court of *parlement*, not to the regulations of the Roman chancery. . . .

13. FROM BERNARD DE GIRARD, SEIGNEUR DU HAILLAN, *De l'Etat et Succès des Affaires de France*, Paris, 1609, Book III, pp. 175 *et seq.*

Concerning the king's majesty, he has complete authority in all matters touching peace and war: he convenes and holds assemblies of the estates of the kingdom, according to the ancient custom of this land, when he considers it necessary: he appoints to all elective offices and benefices and confers governorships, captaincies, the offices of Constable, Chancellor, Marshal, Admiral, Master of the Horse, in short all the offices of the crown and other titles, positions, ranks and honours, military and judicial as well as those appertaining to service in the royal household and which are not venal. He has cognizance in the last resort of the decisions of all magistrates, he appoints or removes all office-holders, imposes upon his subjects, or exempts them from taxes and subsidies, concedes favours and dispensations from the rigour of the laws, raises or lowers the standard, value and base of the currency. . . . In the whole of the kingdom he alone confers letters of favour, of remission, of pardon, of legitimization, of citizenship, letters authorizing the levying of funds and subscriptions, granting hunting rights, permitting the holding of fairs and markets, conferring nobility. He alone can create offices and coin money and he only has the power to reserve for his judges and officers the cognizance of certain crimes, to the number of twenty-four, which we call *cas royaux*. In addition, he alone may dispose of the money in the Exchequer, putting it to whatever public purpose he deems necessary. . . . Only the king makes and interprets laws, sends ambassadors to foreign countries usually to reside there but sometimes to settle a dispute, to negotiate a peace or truce, to make remonstrances or demands, tasks for which the king issues instructions signed by himself and by one of his secretaries of state. He sends condolences on the death of one prince and congratulations on the accession of another; he communicates personally with foreign ambassadors, bestows honours and rewards. Yet although he has absolute authority in all these matters, he does, or ought to do, very little without the advice of his council: and very often what he has declared, given and conceded, is revoked, annulled and rescinded by the authority of that body. . . .

As for these councils, their names and structure have been diverse, according to varying royal dispositions and changing times. Our first kings called their councils *parlements* and they were composed of princes and lords and the most noble dignitaries of the kingdom: all matters were dealt with by this body, whether concerning the state, finance and justice or the suits and quarrels of individuals. Then, as the volume of business began to increase, it became impossible to cope with all the decision-making in these councils called *parlements* and consequently Philip the Fair built the *Palais de Justice* in Paris and there installed a number of councillors who were to have cognizance over civil and criminal actions between individuals ... the king's principal council is a secret one, called the council *d'affaires* ... to which he summons a small number of those whom he reckons to be among the wisest, most experienced and loyal men or of whom he is most fond. To them he communicates the chief matters of state. In this council the letters of ambassadors, governors and frontier captains are read and the contents of despatches to be drawn up by the secretaries of state are decided upon, gifts and favours bestowed, and the documents and despatches from this body are seen and signed by the king....

After the convening of the Estates had been instituted, our kings began to summon them frequently, undertaking no great enterprise without consulting them, in imitation of the first kings who assembled *parlements* in order to decide matters of consequence. Meetings of the Estates serve the same purpose as meetings of the *parlement* did formerly: they allow the king to communicate with his subjects on issues of great importance, to receive their opinions and counsel, to hear their complaints and grievances and also to provide them with answers.

14 (a). FROM J. MASSELIN, *Journal des Etats-Généraux de France tenus à Tours en 1484*, ed. A. Bernier, Paris, 1835, pp. 53–5. The opening address of the Chancellor, Guillaume de Rochfort.

The king ... has determined to enquire directly and through his representatives, and chiefly to hear from your own lips ... what abuses and vices disfigure and injure the general and particular state of the nation.... In fact, he is endeavouring, through your wisdom and probity, to set everything in order.... Let it not cross your mind that your remonstrances will be in vain and your opinions of no account. I assure you that the king will countenance and assent to your advice. Nor will he simply seek to humour you: he will vigorously and constantly pursue those of your suggestions which are beneficial to his own position and to the kingdom, and see that they remain effective.

14 (b). FROM E. MAUGIS, *Histoire du Parlement de Paris de l'Avènement des Rois Valois à la Mort d'Henri IV*, Paris, 1913–16, vol. II, p. 260.

In 1596, Henry IV decided to summon an Assembly of Notables, and in a royal letter, dated July 2, 1596, he informed the *parlement* to that effect.

Having decided to convene a notable assembly of the principal figures of the kingdom to give advice on the welfare and preservation of this State, we have no wish to leave out your opinions and we wish to inform you therefore that if you have anything to tell us which you know to be to the welfare of our office, we will listen in good part and will gladly take account of it.

14 (c). FROM P. R. DOOLIN, *The Fronde*, pp. 78–9, Royal Declaration of July 31, 1648.

As there is nothing which does more to maintain and preserve monarchies in their perfection than the observance of good laws, it is the duty of a great prince to take care for the welfare and the salvation of his subjects, lest they be corrupted by the abuses which creep unobserved into the most perfect states, so as to avoid the ruin which might occur if by negligence the evils became so powerful that they should be unable to support the remedies. Therefore the Kings our predecessors, to prevent these accidents, which cause often the destruction of the most powerful monarchies, have from time to time convoked assemblies to discover and recognize the imperfections and disorders which have been formed in their states, and to advise the best means to remove them. And these assemblies, whether of estates or notables, have always been convoked and regulated by them, since by the law of the kingdom nobody can be established to take cognizance of the government and administration of the monarchy except by the authority and power of the King; and so these assemblies, as they are summoned by the sovereigns, after they have recognized the abuses which it was necessary to correct, and when they have advised the best means to correct them, have always presented to the Kings the *cahiers* of their remonstrances to serve them as matter to make laws and ordinances as they judge best, which are then sent to the sovereign companies, established principally to authorize the justice of the acts of the King, and to cause them to be received by the people with the respect and veneration which is their due. . . .

14 (d). FROM O. RANUM, *Richelieu and the Counsellors of Louis XIII*, Oxford, 1963, p. 16, Claude le Bouthillier to Richelieu, 1642.

I saw by a letter of Monsieur de Noyers to Monsieur the Chancellor that the king was displeased that we created [the office] of provosts generals for the provinces *en son conseil* without talking about it to his Majesty. His Eminence will remember, if it pleases him, that I gave myself the honour of talking to him about it. . . .

(ii). The Three Estates

15 (a). FROM PIERRE DE BOURDEILLE, SEIGNEUR DE BRANTÔME, *Oeuvres Complètes*, ed. L. Lalanne, Paris, 1867, vol. III, pp. 107 *et seq.*

Moreover, this great king [Francis I] bearing in mind the services normally rendered to him by the nobility, and unable to recompense them with money from his domain or from his revenues because of the need to meet the costs of his long, expensive wars, hit upon a means of rewarding those who had served him well, by granting them abbeys and church property instead of leaving them in the hands of useless people, cloistered monks. . . . Now we must commend our great king Henry IV and acknowledge the great debt which the nobility of this kingdom owes to him for not minding the clamour and bawling of members of the clergy as they seek to deprive the nobility of abbeys and church property, to appropriate them all for themselves and leave the nobility far behind. . . . His Majesty has judged accurately that gallant French gentlemen of noble extraction and great merit who hold conscientiousness and honour in such esteem know how to manage and maintain the ecclesiastical rewards bestowed upon them by the king as well or better than any number of churchmen of my acquaintance. . . .

15 (b). FROM E. SPANHEIM, *Relation de la Cour de France en 1690*, ed. E. Bourgeois, Paris, 1900, pp. 453–4.

. . . . the king's right to nominate to benefices . . . not only permits him to give considerable rewards to those whom he considers worthy, but also to recompense through their children the fathers' services in government, finance, justice, war or in service at court in the king's own household. . . .

16 (a). FROM SAINT-SIMON, DUC DE, *Mémoires*, ed. A. de Boislisle, Paris, 1879–1928, vol. XXV, pp. 210–1.

Helped by the ignorance and stupidity of laymen the Church at that time reached the point of assuming all temporal authority through the misuse of the fear inspired by the spiritual power. One can envisage no other period for the obscure origin of the peerages which were attached with ducal titles to the sees of Rheims, Laon and Langres and with the title of count to those of Beauvais, Châlons and Noyon. . . . However, when lay lords learned to read and came to their senses and their vassals did likewise they claimed back what the Church had usurped and though it kept what it could of its gains it was stripped of much of the power and authority which it had formerly wielded. With the elimination of ecclesiastical abuses only the incumbents of those six sees kept their status, their functions, their legislative and constitutive powers in their entirety and remained at the head of the greatest, most powerful and most exalted lords in the kingdom, a position uniquely dependent upon their title of peer.

16 (b). FROM *Recueil des Actes, Titres et Mémoires concernant les Affaires du Clergé de France,* Paris, 1771, vol. III, p. 1098. Decree of the *Grand Conseil,* September 1641.

... *Maître* Bizian Array, a priest and a doctor in theology from the University of Paris, is the lecturer in Divinity in the church of Lyons ... according to the canonical constitution the holder of this theological office ... should enjoy all the profits and revenues of a canonry and prebend in the church of Lyons ... the said Array is not, and cannot, be a member of the chapter because he is unable to prove four generations of nobility either on his father's or his mother's side....

16 (c). FROM VOLTAIRE, *Dictionnaire Philosophique,* ed. R. Naves, Paris, 1954, pp. 85–6. *Catéchisme du Curé,* 1764.

Ariston: So, my dear Téotine, you intend to become a country *curé?*

Téotine: Yes. I am to have a small parish which I would prefer to a large one. I have only a limited amount of intelligence and cleverness; I certainly couldn't guide seventy thousand souls seeing that I possess only one; a large flock would frighten me but I can do some good with a small one. I have studied some jurisprudence and will endeavour to the best of my ability to prevent my poor parishioners from being ruined by lawsuits. I know enough medicine to suggest simple remedies when they are ill. I know enough about agriculture to give them useful advice on occasion. The lord of the manor and his lady are decent moderate people, who will help me to perform my work well. I expect to live contentedly enough and I believe people will be content with me.

Ariston: Are you not displeased that you cannot have a wife? ... it would be pleasant if, after preaching, chanting, hearing confessions, celebrating communion, baptising, burying, comforting the sick, patching up quarrels, spending the whole day serving your fellow creatures, you could come home to a gentle, agreeable and virtuous wife....

17. FROM *Recueil des Actes, Titres et Mémoires concernant les Affaires du Clergé de France*, vol. IX, pp. 3–8.

Contract of Poissy, 1561.

... during the next six years, commencing on 1 January, 1561 and ending on the last day of December 1567, the deputies of the Clergy will raise by tithes and by other means, according to their own judgment, the sum of sixteen hundred thousand *livres* ... payable in half-yearly sums of eight hundred thousand *livres* on the last days of March and September. The collection of this money will be in the hands of whomever the Clergy decide to nominate, without the king having to bear any of the expenses, and these deputies will be responsible for the conversion of eighty thousand *livres* from each half-yearly quota for the discharge and redemption of domanial dues, *aides*, salt taxes and state investments, in conformity with the estimates approved annually by the king's Privy Council and despatched to the *trésoriers de France* and to the collectors-general of finance ... for his part, the king promises and grants that in return for the sixteen hundred thousand *livres* he will not levy from the Clergy any tenths, *francs-fiefs*, purchase taxes, loans or *dons gratuits* and he will maintain and preserve the Clergy individually and as a whole in the possession of that property which each and every member of the Clergy currently holds and was held in the past by their clerical predecessors.

18 (a). FROM IBID., vol. VIII, pp. 10–12.

Extract from a letter of the Assembly of Clergy for the provinces, 1595.

The General Assembly of the clergy, meeting in the years 1579 and 1580 saw fit to draw up a regulation for the conduct of affairs which it seems right should be maintained and inserted here on this occasion ... the prelates and deputies meeting in that Assembly judged it necessary to appoint two agents from their number who would stay behind in Paris after the conclusion of the meeting ... their task would be carefully and diligently to guard against any innovation which might be prejudicial to the Clergy, to the *Cahier* and royal letters-patent drawn up in the Clergy's favour, or to the articles, contracts and agreements negotiated with his Majesty; to safeguard and ensure the execution of these arrangements these agents would speak out when necessary, representing to his Majesty, to the members of his Privy Council and to anybody else concerned what to them seemed in the Clergy's interests, to its credit, for its well-being, relief and benefit, and they would warn the Archbishops or metropolitan syndics of any proposals that threatened the contrary, doing everything in their power to resist such proposals.

G

18 (b). FROM IBID., vol. XIII, pp. 242–3.

Remonstrances of the French Clergy to Henry IV, May 1596, made by the Bishop of Le Mans.

The favourable regulations by which the Church was formerly governed, the piety, doctrine and apt discourses of our predecessors, the task which they performed in their official capacity of instructing the people by word and example, all these factors have given our order abundant temporal wealth, out of which it has been possible to grant assistance to the secular power, something that has been done on a number of occasions, without limiting the funds necessary for the maintenance of the divine office or the livelihood of those called to celebrate it. In the last thirty years this wealth has been diminished by more than three quarters; indeed, it would be no exaggeration to say that in the last ten years alone, without taking previous losses into account, we have lost virtually that amount. This loss may be demonstrated easily enough. Our chief and most obvious form of income is that derived from tenths levied on the profits from our land, over half of which is at present lying fallow and the remainder is so badly cultivated that it no longer brings in what it formerly did. Besides, in a number of places people are only paying tenths when the fancy takes them and a great many people of all ranks are paying nothing at all. Others are wrongfully seizing and making free with them, so that our impoverishment in this respect is thoroughly evident. Moreover, of the lands and possessions which we had and which remained ours after three or four previous alienations, a large proportion was sold in the years 1586 and 1588 to support the kingdom; and the little remaining has been so ruined and pillaged by soldiers, and our farmers so badly treated, that nobody is willing to farm and till the land, except at much reduced rents, whilst a number of areas remain entirely barren. The mass of the people, whose charity and generosity have given us so much help and relief, are so impoverished that we can expect very little more help from them; at the same time our expenses have grown rather than decreased. We have to rebuild or replace churches, church furniture, ornaments, chalices, books and other things necessary to celebrate the divine office, rebuild and repair our houses in town and country, and all this at a time when prices have doubled.

Our growing impoverishment gives us a just and valid motive for asking to be released from the subsidy accorded to your royal predecessor—may God absolve him—in 1584 and 1586. Yet in view of your Majesty's great needs and the expenses that you have to sustain, and because it is right that your subjects should strive to help you, we have not in fact objected to granting the same subsidy for a further ten years, and we have signed a contract to that effect with members of your council; we will do all in our power to fulfil our part of the contract. But to a large extent that will depend upon the success of our main aim, namely the re-establishment of discipline in our ranks ... so that benefices may go to worthy and fitting incumbents and not to laymen holding them in trust and drawing revenue from them, at the same time withholding taxes intended both for the maintenance of the divine office and for the payment of this subsidy to the state.

18 (c). FROM IBID., vol. XIII, p. 451.
Remonstrances of the Clergy to Louis XIII, May 1625, by the Archbishop of Bordeaux.

We have assembled here [in Paris] at your Majesty's command, conveyed to us by our agents, in accordance with the terms of the contracts signed by you, Sire, and ourselves, by which you permit us ... to assemble in order to consider among ourselves temporal as well as spiritual matters, including a statement from our controller of accounts ... if your Majesty wishes us to remain, it must be with the same freedom as we have previously enjoyed; the dioceses and provinces must be allowed to send whichever deputies they please and if a contract is to be signed with your Majesty they must have complete freedom in the matter of voting.

19. FROM *Cahiers des états de Normandie*, 1633–1666, ed. C. de R. de Beaurepaire, Rouen, 1878, XXXVII, pp. 105–6.
Cahiers of November 1643.

In order to guarantee more readily the profits of the tax-farmer in the *généralité* of Rouen, the *intendants* of justice, commissioners who are neither recognized as officials in the ordinances of your state nor as judges by the laws of your kingdom, but who are ministers sent to carry out orders in your Majesty's name, have scandalously subjected priests to payment of the *taille*, despite the immunity accorded by their sacred character ... ; the Church complains against this treatment and implores the restoration of its liberty which your predecessors have never denied it, entreating you to annul these impositions and to preserve all the rights and privileges which the Church has enjoyed in the past.
The king's annotated reply in council: The ordinances, decrees and regulations issued on this subject will be observed, kept and executed.

20 (a). FROM *Recueil des Actes, Titres et Mémoires concernant les Affaires du Clergé de France*, vol. VII, p. 370.
Ordinance of August 1539.

... without prejudice to temporal and secular jurisdiction in cases involving clergymen who carry on professions or trades which have customarily made them accountable to secular courts in both civil and criminal matters. . . .

20 (b). FROM IBID., vol. VI, p. 70.
Ordinance of 1610.

It is our will that when our officers seek to claim cognizance directly or indirectly by means of possessory actions, formal complaint or appeal *en nouvelleté*[1] over any spiritual matters, whether involving the sacraments, the office, management or discipline of the church, or disputes between clerics, those ordinances of previous kings which have assigned to our officers what is their proper sphere and also determined the bounds of ecclesiastical jurisdiction shall be observed, so that each side performs its duty, keeping within the prescribed limits and not encroaching upon the other's area of influence. We expressly forbid such encroachments. We also charge our *parlements* to allow the ecclesiastical courts to handle cases within their competence, those concerning the sacraments and other purely spiritual and ecclesiastical matters, and not to take them over on a possessory plea or on any other pretext.

20 (c). FROM IBID., vol. VI, pp. 218–19. Royal declaration of February 1657.

In accordance with our ordinances, we forbid our *parlements* or any of our judges to take cognizance of charges brought against any clerics either secular or regular, whether priest, deacon or sub-deacon, or against the holders of benefices or against anyone who has taken religious vows, except in those privileged cases specified in the ordinances.

20 (d). FROM IBID., vol. XIII, pp. 663–5.
Remonstrances of the Clergy to Louis XIV, May 1657, by the Archbishop of Bordeaux.

Our immunities are sublime qualities which we have received from

---

[1] The appeal *en cas de saisine et nouvelleté* allowed clerics to seek redress in royal courts in matters relating to the possession of ecclesiastical rights or property.

God and not through the generosity of man; they are bright adornments enhancing the lustre of that dignity which all ecclesiastics possess, which is inseparable from our state and which is one of the chief embellishments of the episcopacy.

Yet, although these august marks of godliness that make clerics the object of the peoples' respect and veneration are ours by divine right, they are often treated with contempt and injustice by the very people who ought to respect them and who have an obligation to defend them.

As far as our exemptions and privileges are concerned they must be weighed against the heavy sacrifices made in paying the immense sums that the Clergy has granted from time to time and without obligation to your Majesty and to his royal predecessors because of their needs and those of the state; they are evidently no longer of any account. . . .

This is not to say that we no longer hope that your Majesty's sense of goodness and justice will persuade him to re-establish our rights in their entirety, especially since we already have various proofs of it in his declarations and decrees, like the one confirming that the *régale* would not apply to those churches which have not been subjected to it previously. The same may be said of those privileges and exemptions concerning ecclesiastical property, for which, in response to the humble pleas of the General Assembly, the king has granted declaratory letters. May we mention one more action, Sire, worthy of your Majesty's piety, which cannot be too highly praised, relating as it does to the preservation of the personal immunities of the cardinals, archbishops and bishops of your kingdom; such an act causes us to hope that you may see fit to complete so glorious and godly a task by re-establishing the immunities of clerics of the second order.

Having humbly thanked your Majesty for his support in this important area, we beg him to permit us to say that at present we are unhappily forced to witness a host of disturbances in the sphere of ecclesiastical discipline and in our dioceses as a result of continual encroachments by your *parlements* and magistrates upon our area of jurisdiction; they do not merely prevent us from suppressing crime, they actually facilitate it through the machinery of the appeal *comme d'abus*,[1] a fact which obliged previous assemblies of the clergy to complain and which today forces us to point out to your Majesty that this appeal is now so excessively employed that vice flourishes unpunished and virtue is held in scorn; ecclesiastical authority has been almost totally destroyed. Secular judges have laid profane hands upon the spiritual power, they have peered into the holy of holies. They affect cognizance of purely spiritual matters; they regulate the divine

[1] A complaint to a *parlement* against an ecclesiastical judge accused of exceeding his powers.

office; they give orders and lift censures as they please; they make pronouncements on religious vows; they authorize *curés* and preachers; and they even pass judgement on the validity of our sacraments.

21 (a). FROM G. DE LA ROQUE, *Traité de la Noblesse,* new edn., Rouen, 1735, pp. 270–1.

Noblemen and those enjoying personal nobility have a great many privileges which non-nobles do not possess. Unlike the *roturiers* they may bear their own coats of arms . . . there are benefices and ecclesiastical honours which can only be held by noblemen. . . . The *noblesse de race* and those possessing personal nobility are exempt from payment of the *taille*, the *aides* and the various additional subsidies, impositions and supplies . . . with the exception of Dauphiné, Provence and Languedoc where the system of the *taille réelle*, depending on the quality of the land and not of the individual, is in force. . . . Fiefs and seigneuries have long been the preserve of the nobility, *roturiers* requiring a special dispensation. . . . A nobleman is not obliged to billet soldiers, he may carry a sword, hunt and shoot. . . . If in debt, he is not liable to be flogged; but he can be beheaded for treason, robbery, perjury and the giving of false evidence, for his rank aggravates and augments his crime . . . noblemen are severely punished through fines and financial penalties.

21 (b). FROM *Cahiers des états de Normandie,* XXXVIII, November, 1643.

The tax-farmers have treated the nobility in a strange fashion . . . they have sought to attach noble immunity to a single area within whose boundaries alone could the nobleman assert his privileges, so that he would be allowed to cultivate only one of his estates without paying the *taille,* as if the *taille réelle* was the rule in Normandy, as if an individual possessing personal immunity and exemption could catch some stain of common servitude from cultivating other parts of the property with which God had endowed him, as if his rank changed every time he moved from one part of his land to another, a commoner in this part, a nobleman in the other. This abuse has been directed against the Church as well as against the nobility, for clerics have been forbidden to cultivate more than one of their estates, as if they became laymen subject to the *taille,* in moving from one to the other. This initiative provides a very dangerous precedent which could have most injurious consequences for the whole province, and the churches and nobility of this province entreat you to preserve the ancient customs so that these two orders, who have not deserved less from the state than their predecessors, whose freedom to dispose of their own property has never been contradicted, may no longer be submitted to such ill-treatment.

The king's annotated reply in council: The *intendants,* as they proceed with the levying of *tailles,* will observe the edicts and regulations issued on this subject.

21 (c). FROM L. CHÉRIN, *Abrégé Chronologique d'Edits, Déclarations, Règlements, Arrêts et Lettres Patentes des Rois de France de la Troisième Race concernant le Fait de Noblesse,* Paris, 1788. Declaration of December, 1485.

Gold and silver cloth, silk robes or linings may be worn only by members of the nobility, living nobly and representing ancient noble families which have never been subject to forfeiture. They may wear silk in accordance with the following rules: knights with an income of 2,000 *livres* may wear silk cloth of any kind, and esquires with a similar income may wear damask cloth and figured satin, but not velvet, whether crimson or of another hue.

22. FROM G. DE LA ROQUE, *Traité de la Noblesse,* pp. 29–31.

Noblesse de race is acquired in a certain number of stages. . . . Enoblement bestows nobility but not *noblesse de race.* . . . Jean Baquet relates five methods by which members of the latter group may be identified. First, if their forefathers were deemed to be noblemen—in the event of forfeiture subsequent generations had to fulfil the stages stipulated above—and if they bore the noble title of esquire or knight. Secondly, if they lived nobly and dressed in a manner befitting their status . . . thirdly, if their father and grandfather had borne arms or held offices worthy of the nobility, like those of bailiff and seneschal. Fourthly, if their forefathers had possessed country estates, exercised judicial manorial authority, owned fiefs. Fifthly, if they bore coats of arms which adorned their churches and tombs. To these should be added those families which from time to time have received declaratory judgments confirming their nobility, based on title-deeds, or on the deposition of irreproachable witnesses who have a thorough knowledge of the case. . . . Finally, a distinction needs to be made between those who can relinquish their nobility and those who cannot. The *noblesse de race* cannot do so except tacitly as a result of forfeiture. On the other hand those possessing only personal nobility may be allowed to, because their status does not depend upon their predecessors, and this is a matter, therefore, of *jus quaesitum.*

23. FROM IBID., pp. 54–5.

Usually one reckons seven means whereby nobility may be acquired in France. The most ancient applies to the feudal nobility, those families which once served the king as soldiers in defence of the realm. The second involves the bestowal of knighthood which requires no other ceremony than the royal accolade, if conferred just before battle; it may be bestowed on other occasions in whatever fashion the sovereign wishes, or it may be acquired by virtue of admission to a military order, based on statute. The third is by mayoralty, when the king rewards those men who administer towns and communities, and have given generous service. The fourth refers to the illegitimate descendants of members of the feudal nobility, whose nobility is in recognition of the services of their natural fathers. The fifth means is by acquisition of the office of royal secretary, which is considered to confer immediate hereditary nobility. The sixth is the adventitious result of exercising certain offices and posts. This means is external, accessory and indirect, and may be called gradual since its origin is in one generation and its final establishment in another. But as a safeguard this form of nobility is amenable to declaratory or corroboratory letters. The seventh originates in specific letters, or in royal edicts and declarations, or in general charters.

To put the matter more neatly by a more concise division we may say that there are only two kinds of nobility. The first is nobility by birth, nobility depending upon noble ancestry; the second is nobility bestowed by the prince when he chooses to acknowledge the quality and merits of those who have rended him some great service by honouring them and their issue with the title of noblemen.

24 (a). FROM L. CHÉRIN, *Abrégé Chronologique d'Edits, Déclarations, Règlements, Arrêts et Lettres Patentes des Rois de France de la Troisième Race concernant le Fait de Noblesse.*
Edict on the *Taille*, March 1600.

The license and corruption of the times has provided the opportunity for some men, under the pretext of having carried arms during the recent troubles, to usurp the rank of nobleman in order to gain exemption improperly from payment of the *taille*. To remedy this abuse his Majesty hereby forbids anyone to take the title of esquire and place himself in the ranks of the nobility who is not descended from a grandfather and father who have given distinguished military service, or have given public service in one of those honourable offices which according to the laws and customs of this kingdom may provide a starting point for the acquisition of nobility. Even in such cases it is necessary that the grandfather and father should have lived in a manner befitting their quality, committing no degrading acts, and that their son should follow their example, otherwise he will be ignominously deprived of a title which he has no right to profess.

24 (b). FROM IBID., Edict of Louis XIV, July 1644.

The presidents, counsellors, *avocat-général* and *procureur-général*, the chief clerk and the four notaries and secretaries of the *Parlement* of Paris and their successors in these offices are hereby declared noblemen, and his Majesty further stipulates that the said office-holders, their widows during widowhood and their descendants, male and female, born and yet to be born, will enjoy all the privileges and distinctions accorded to noblemen, barons and gentlemen of this kingdom, even though they are not descended from ancient noble lines, provided that the said office-holders will have served for twenty years and will still hold the office at the time of their death.

25 (a). FROM IBID., Letters-Patent of Charles VIII, February, 1484.

This prince hereby confirms all the privileges accorded by preceding kings to the clerks, notaries and secretaries of the royal household; he ennobles them where necessary, together with their children and their issue, male and female, born and yet to be born in legitimate wedlock; he declares them fit to receive any order of chivalry as if their nobility was ancient, in excess of four generations: all this without any cash payment.

25 (b). FROM IBID., Letters of Charles VIII, April 1491.

The privilege of nobility is hereby confirmed in favour of the mayor and aldermen of Bourges, the number of aldermen being reduced to four. The mayor must be a native of Bourges; his nobility and that of the aldermen is subject to forfeiture if any of them or of their issue act in a manner unworthy of their status, as by indulging in trade and commerce or exercising the offices of notary or solicitor.

25 (c). FROM IBID., Letters-Patent of Francis I, 1536.

This prince hereby ennobles the mayor and the four aldermen of Péronne, in recognition of the courageous defence of the town by its inhabitants when, in the course of a year, it was besieged and then bombarded by sixty cannon from the army of the Emperor Charles V under the command of the counts of Nassau and Reux, who were forced eventually to lift the siege.

25 (d). FROM IBID., Edict of January 1568.

In return for cash his Majesty will ennoble twelve individuals to be named by him, who will themselves enjoy, as will their issue, male and female, born and yet to be born in legal wedlock, all the privileges of noblemen of this kingdom, just as if they were descended from an ancient noble line.

25 (e). FROM G. DE LA ROQUE, Traité de la Noblesse, p. 201.

The Estates-General assembled in Paris in 1614–15, pointed out to king Louis XIII (article 171 of their remonstrances) that the title of nobility which was once accorded only to persons of great merit and as a reward for courageous acts could now be obtained in return for money, or simply as a mark of grace and favour, something which aroused the contempt of the ancient nobility and of the great mass of the people who bore the weight of this excessively large noble class. In order to eliminate this evil the Estates begged the king not to issue letters of nobility in the future, save to those who had given long and conspicuous service to the state and to the public.

26 (a). FROM L. CHÉRIN, Abrégé Chronologique d'Edits, Déclarations, Règlements, Arrêts et Lettres Patentes des Rois de France de la Troisième Race concernant le Fait de Noblesse, Declaration of Francis I, October 1546.

Those who call themselves noblemen without being able to prove their title will be made subject to the taille and to the customary subsidies.

26 (b). FROM IBID. Extract from a letter concerning the usurpation of the title of nobility addressed by Dom Louis de Requesens, governor in Artois, to the president and councillors of the supreme council of Artois, February 17, 1576.

Certain abuses are being perpetrated today in the towns and villages of the country and county of Artois; that is to say that a large number of people who are not nobles and are of very low rank are taking and usurping the titles of nobleman or esquire, putting themselves forward and styling themselves as such among the noblemen and squires of this part of the country, and under the shelter of these titles, aspiring to exemptions and freedoms in order to avoid paying the contributions to the tailles and the aides which roturiers owe to the king.

Since cognizance of these matters rests with the élus of Artois, they have been ordered to inquire into the activities of these usurpers so that that the *procureur-général* of the *élection* may indict them before the *élus* who can take judicial action against them so that these abuses may be extirpated and this license, which is prejudicial to His Majesty and to his subjects, may be checked; and because the fault appears to proceed in part from the notaries, the *élus* have been commanded to forbid them in the future to allow such titles of esquire and nobleman if they have no knowledge of their being merited, of the persons concerned living as noblemen and being reputed as such.

His Majesty orders the president and members of the council of Artois to summon the *élus* to meet them so that together they may consider how best to eliminate such abuses and ensure the observance of these regulations aimed chiefly against notaries and public persons who approve contracts in which they list such titles vaguely and without exercising judgment, which ill becomes them; and especially [he orders the president and members of the council] to act themselves against them in accordance with their own procedure should difficulties arise over the jurisdiction of the *élus* in this matter.

26 (c). FROM IBID.
Extract from the *Cahiers des Remontrances*, presented by the nobility during the Estates-General meeting of 1614.

His Majesty is most humbly entreated to ensure ... that those who have taken advantage of the times to give themselves unjustly the title of nobleman and to enjoy the privileges appertaining thereto should be deprived of their title and declared *roturiers*; and so that non-nobles should not infiltrate into the ranks of the nobility an exact register should be drawn up of all the noblemen in the kingdom, together with their coats of arms and an account of the honours and ancient lineage of their families. ... In future letters of knighthood should be bestowed only upon persons of worth whose public service greatly merits such a reward ... it should be lawful for the nobility to take part in wholsesale trading without forfeiture of nobility, this without prejudice to the custom of Brittany. Also, only noblemen ought to hold the rank of port-captain.

26 (d). FROM IBID.,
Edict of Louis XIII, January 1634.

We forbid any of our subjects to usurp the status of nobility, to take the title of esquire and to bear coats of arms if they are not of a noble house and extraction, under pain of a fine of 2,000 *livres*.

26 (e). FROM R. MOUSNIER, J. P. LABATUT, Y. DURAND, *Deux Cahiers de la Noblesse*, Paris, 1965, p. 141.

Cahier des Remontrances de la Noblesse du Bailliage de Troyes, 1651, Articles 26–28.

[We ask that] all *roturiers* should be forbidden to take and usurp the rank of esquire, to adopt and bear crested coats of arms, and other titles and marks appertaining to true members of the *noblesse de race;* and women who are *roturières* and the wives of *roturiers* should be forbidden to take the rank of gentlewomen. . . .

All those who have themselves or whose predecessors have usurped the rank of esquire and adopted crested coats of arms should be commanded to renounce them, and their crests and coats of arms and other marks and titles belonging to true noblemen should be removed from whatever places they may be found in, including churches, under pain of a fine of two thousand *livres.* . . .

All persons should be forbidden to change their family name and to adopt as their name that of an area of land and they should also be forbidden to take the names and coats of arms of other families under pain of a fine of two thousand *livres.*

27. FROM G. DE LA ROQUE, *Traité du Ban et Arrière-Ban,* chapter IV, pp. 10–11.

Noblemen have served in the armies of France for a long time. . . . However, so too have *roturiers* and for a long time all those who possessed fiefs, irrespective of the conditions of ownership, attended the *ban et arrière-ban.* . . . King Louis XI sanctioned the privilege of members of the third estate to hold fiefs, in letters-patent issued at Rouen on 13 June, 1467. In an edict of 1470 he ordered all those holding fiefs to attend the *arrière-bans* in person and with their arms, forbidding them to send anybody in their place under pain of forfeiture of life and property. Yet it seemed invidious to this prince that non-nobles should possess fiefs and in the same year, in letters issued at Plessis les Tours, he ennobled all non-nobles who held fiefs in Normandy . . . in order that these men should serve the state with a more appropriate rank, alongside the rest of the nobility.

28 (a). FROM A. BELLEGUISE, *Traité de la Noblesse et de son Origine, suivant les Préjugés rendus par les Commissaires députés pour la Vérification des Titres de Noblesse,* Paris, 1700, chapter VI.

Like all other worldly possessions, nobility is vulnerable to misfortune; poverty tarnishes it when a nobleman is forced to become a craftsman. Under the duress of harsh necessity it may seem that the nobleman who has accepted the implications of his misfortune should have the right to regain his status automatically once the cause of his forfeiture has been removed, since his nobility has not been entirely destroyed but rather has suffered a kind of eclipse which is removed with the return of more prosperous times. Some authors have argued along these lines to the effect that letters of rehabilitation are not necessary. Yet since a change of luck has no connection with one's sensibilities and since a lowering of one's station always has some adverse effects, it is necessary for the prince, through the exercise of his authority, to blot out the stain and provide authentic and public testimony that his subject is no longer in a degraded condition.

Besides, necessity is not always the reason for forfeiture; the desire for gain makes as many nobles deceitful as misfortune makes needy: so that if it were possible to regain noble status without letters of rehabilitation, some nobles might become *roturiers* for perhaps a month, reverting in the following month to their previous rank. In order to miss no opportunity for advancing their own interests, they would change their status as readily as their mode of dress; it is certain, therefore, that letters of rehabilitation are necessary.

28 (b). FROM IBID., chapter V.

It is unquestionable that the practice of all mechanical arts, with the exception of glass-making, causes forfeiture of nobility: the reason being that the assiduity of the craftsmen's daily labour and the desire to make enough money to live on makes them like slaves, instilling in them only feelings of baseness and subjection, incompatible with the sentiments of a true nobleman. . . .

28 (c). FROM L. CHÉRIN, *Abrégé Chronologique d'Edits, Déclarations, Règlements, Arrêts et Lettres Patentes des Rois de France de la Troisième Race concernant le Fait de Noblesse.*
Edict of Charles IX, 1560.

All noblemen are forbidden to take part in trade or in tax-farming, either directly or through an intermediary, under pain of deprivation of noble privileges and liability for the *taille*; and for office-holders, deprivation of their office.

28 (d). FROM G. DE LA ROQUE, *Traité de la Noblesse*, p. 256, Ordinance of January, 1629.

In order to urge our subjects, of whatever quality and condition they may be, to apply themselves to maritime trade and commerce, we wish that our intention to elevate and honour those who do so may be made known. We ordain that all noblemen who directly or through intermediaries, take out shares or become partners in ships, commodities and merchandise appertaining to this trade, will retain their nobility, though they may not take part in retail trading nor will they be exempt from the taxes, duties and impositions which have to be paid for the import, export and passage of such commodities and merchandise.

29 (a). FROM C. LOYSEAU, *Traité des Ordres*, Paris, 1613, pp. 92–3, chapter VIII.

Strictly speaking, the term *bourgeois* does not include all the inhabitants of the towns. For members of the nobility who set up house in town do not qualify as *bourgeois* since the order of nobility is quite separate from the third estate, to which the *bourgeoisie* belong. That is why the terms *bourgeois* and noble are normally contrasted, as when one speaks of [a town's] noble and *bourgeois* guard. In addition, the wretched representatives of the lower classes have no right to call themselves *bourgeois:* they have no share therefore in the honours of the city and no voice in its assemblies, which are the preserve of the *bourgeoisie.*

It is not even accurate to say that members of the *bourgeoisie* are to be found in all towns; they only belong in privileged towns which have corporative and communal rights. For to be a citizen or a *bourgeois*... is to have a share in the rights and privileges of a city: so that if a city has no corporation and municipal council, no officials and privileges, it cannot contain members of the *bourgeoisie*...as Bodin observes...in our tongue, *bourgeois* implies something even more special than citizen.

29 (b). FROM *Ordonnances des Rois de France de la Troisième Race*, Paris, 1814, vol. XVI, pp. 425–6, An edict exempting the *bourgeois* of Paris from the obligation to billet soldiers, October 1465.

Louis, by the grace of God, King of France. Be it known to all at this time and in the future that our fine town and city of Paris, the chief and most important town in our kingdom, has received a number of valuable rights, privileges, prerogatives and pre-eminences and gained recognition of certain customs and practices from our predecessors which none of the other towns in our kingdom have acquired, including the immemorial right of the *bourgeois* of this city to be exempted from the obligation of billetting in the city our officers, soldiers or any other persons, either through the agency of quartermasters or in any other way, if they do not wish to do so. Since our joyous accession and first entry into the town and in response to our request, the *bourgeois* have on a number of occasions endured and tolerated the billetting of officers, soldiers and others in their town residences and mansions, sometimes in order to ensure the safety of our person, sometimes to guarantee the defence of the town in time of war or of some other disturbance, not at the discretion of the quartermasters but in accordance with regulations drawn up by our well-beloved mayor and aldermen. The said *bourgeois* fear that these actions may be interpreted in the future as creating a precedent if we do not provide against that possibility, and this they have humbly pointed out to us. Therefore, let it be known that because we do not wish the tolerance which the *bourgeois* have demonstrated in permitting their houses and residences to be used for military accommodation to detract from, or in any way prejudice the rights, customs and immunities which they have enjoyed from time immemorial, we have ratified the said rights, customs and immunities of our *bourgeois*; and through the exercise of our most abundant goodwill, our absolute power and royal authority . . . we have granted, and are granting them anew, the freedom to use their mansions and residences in the said town entirely as they see fit, without any obligation, either at present or in the future, to billet or allow to be billetted officers, soldiers or any other persons whatsoever, either through the agency of quartermasters or in any other way, however expedient it may be, if they do not so wish.

29 (c). FROM IBID., vol. XVI, pp. 434–5, Letters of Louis XI confirming the exemption of the *bourgeois* of Paris from the *ban et arrière-ban* and their freedom from summons before any court outside the city boundaries, November 1465.

Louis, by the grace of God, King of France. Be it know to all at this time and in the future that our fine town and city of Paris is the chief and most important town of our kingdom, worthy of having precedence in privileges, prerogatives and pre-eminences over all the others, both because of the merits of our *bourgeois* subjects and because the town's growth and preservation contributes to our welfare and that of the Crown. Consequently the said *bourgeois* have been maintained heretofore by our predecessors and by us in the custom and practice which prevents them from being dealt with outside the walls and enclosures of Paris, in respect of any kind of summons, misdemeanour or other legal suit of whatever kind it may be, from being under the jurisdiction of any court outside the said walls and enclosures and from pleading anywhere save in the said town. In addition, members of the nobility and other inhabitants of the town who hold fiefs or *arrières-fiefs* in our kingdom are not liable to serve outside the town, following a summons of *ban et arrière-ban*. For our part we recognize the great loyalty which the said *bourgeois* have demonstrated towards us, a loyalty in which we have singular confidence, and in order that the *bourgeois* may always be disposed to remain loyal to us and to our Crown, we have ratified the above mentioned customs and practices. In exercising our most bounteous and abundant good will, our absolute power and royal authority ... we have granted to them and their successors the privilege of not being answerable outside the walls and enclosures of Paris in any legal suit whatever and of pleading only within the said town if they so wish; and to the nobles and *bourgeois* of the said town who possess fiefs and *arrières-fiefs* we concede that they are not in any circumstances obliged to leave the town in answer to a summons of *ban et arrière-ban*, always provided that those holding fiefs or *arrières-fiefs* should maintain sufficiently protective apparel in keeping with the value of their fiefs and *arrières-fiefs*, in order to help to guard and defend our town of Paris. ...

30 (a). FROM IBID., vol. XVI, p. 501, Ratification of an agreement made between the lord and inhabitants of Pierre in Gevaudan for the exercise of certain rights bought by the Commune.

Louis, by the grace of God, King of France. Be it known to all at this time and in the future that we have accepted the humble petition of the attorneys, syndics, peasants and inhabitants of the land and lordship of Pierre in the district of Gevaudan who were formerly obliged to use the ovens belonging to the manor of Pierre and no other and also to mount guard at the gate of the said manor and perform certain other very onerous duties, to discharge themselves from which they paid certain sums of money to the lord of Pierre and his predecessors. Because the payments made by the suppliants and their predecessors diminished the fief and lordship of Pierre, commissioners appointed by us to look into the matter of *francs-fiefs* and new acquisitions[1] in Languedoc, who have been concerned for two years or thereabouts with the affairs of their commission, appreciated our interest in the case of Pierre and persuaded the suppliants to agree to provide the money or indemnity due to us ... in this matter of an indemnity the suppliants have compounded with our commissioners for the sum of eight hundred and twenty five *livres*. ...

---

[1] *Francs-fiefs* and *nouvel acquêt* were both taxes paid to the king, the first by purchasers of fiefs and the second by communities which had acquired new property rights.

30 (b). FROM L. CHÉRIN, *Abrégé Chronologique d'Edits, Déclarations, Règlements, Arrêts et Lettres Patentes des Rois de France de la Troisième Race concernant le Fait de Noblesse.* Edict of July 1576.

All *roturiers* and all who have not been ennobled are hereby forbidden to usurp noble status, either by their titles or dress, nor may the wives of *roturiers* wear the garb of gentlewomen and the finery of velvet.

31. FROM *Chartes de Communes et d'Affranchissements en Bourgogne*, ed. J. Garnier, Dijon, 1877, vol. III, pp. 113–4.
Edict of Henry II, September, 1554, abolishing serfdom in the royal domains of Burgundy.

Henry, by the grace of God, King of France . . . by a perpetual and irrevocable edict, with our certain knowledge, full power and royal authority, we decree, declare and ordain that the condition of mortmain will be obliterated and abolished . . . in the said lands and manors belonging to our domain. . . . It is our will and desire that all men and women born and dwelling in these lands, and native to them . . . who were formerly subject to the custom and condition of mortmain, shall no longer be so; instead with their heirs and issue they shall be free and unconstrained as regards both their persons and property, and they shall remain hereafter in a condition of complete and total liberty, as do our other subjects and *bourgeois* who live in the cities, towns and other free places in our Duchy of Burgundy.

H

B. The Government of the Kingdom

(i). The Subjects' Role

32. FROM *Nouveau Recueil de Registres Domestiques Limousins et Marchois*, ed. L. Guibert, Paris, 1895, vol. I, p. 333.
Journal of N. . . . Vielbans, councillor in the *présidial* court of Brive and a consul of this town.

On the twenty-second day of February, 1584, I was elected first consul of Brive; Sebastien de la Forestie, *seigneur* of La Pascherie was elected second; Jehan Bellet, *bourgeois,* was elected third; and *maître* Guy Devalle, a royal notary, was elected fourth. . . . We were sworn into office on the twenty-fifth of February in the same year, which was a Saturday; at the same time *maître* Etienne Boix, attorney, and Jehan Roche, *bourgeois,* were made syndics of the town. . . On the tenth of April, 1584, I had an appointment in the town hall with the weavers, in order to measure their ells and weights, which I found to be short. On the eleventh of April we ordered all tradesmen to measure with the Parisian ell and maintain a proper weight; likewise we commanded the weavers to recognize only the Parisian ell and the Roman weights: the fine for not observing these regulations was fixed at one hundred *sous.* On the same day it was discovered that the bread in some bakers' shops was of short weight. The list of offenders is in the town hall registry. On the night of the twelfth of April we had our sergeant, Drinon, taken into custody for not having attended the evening procession and not coming to notify me at my home. On the twenty-ninth of May in the same year I exacted a fine of thirty-two testoons[1] from a man who had sold grain before mid-day.

Maître Etienne de Lestang, president and lieutenant-general of our bench, died on Wednesday, the first of April, 1587, between ten and eleven o'clock at night . . . On Monday, the sixth of April, 1587, M. du Vialard was admitted to the office of president and lieutenant-general and on the same day presided over the court. The first case to be heard was an appeal which the president approved, ordering the relevant documents to be communicated to the *gens du roi.*[2]

[1] An old French coin: the total fine came to a little over 3 francs.
[2] The *Procureur-Général* and the *Avocats-Généraux* who were the royal representatives in the *parlements.*

33. FROM *Recueil Des Lois*, ed. F. Isambert, XIII, p. 542, Art. VI, *Royal Declaration on the authority of Bailiffs, Seneschals and Prévôts, June 1559.*

As regards the public assemblies and conventions ... which are composed of our judges and the officials and subjects of our towns and *prévôtés* ... we hereby ordain and will that henceforth such assemblies and debates shall not take place unless our *prévôts* and *châtelains* are summoned there by the usher, serjeant or any other person possessing a writ or mandate to convene the municipal councils of those towns where the *prévôts* and *châtelains* act as the ordinary judges; they will assist the bailiffs and seneschals or their lieutenants in auditing, investigating and closing those accounts which are customarily presented before our officers by the municipal tax collectors, whether concerning communal funds or specific funds raised to cope with some particular situation; and they will assist in any other deliberations, without drawing a salary for so doing. It is also our wish that in the absence of the bailiffs, seneschals or their lieutenant-generals or other subordinates, our *prévôts* and *châtelains* should preside and pass judgement on the accounts submitted to them.

34 (a). FROM IBID., XIV, pp. 208–9.
Ordinance of Moulins, February 1566, Art. 71.

In order to bring some order to the administration of the towns in our kingdom and attend to the complaints which we have received in this matter, we have ordained that the mayors, aldermen, consuls, *capitouls* and administrators of town councils who have had in the past and at present have jurisdiction over civil, criminal and police affairs shall in the future only retain jurisdiction over criminal and police matters, to which we direct them to devote themselves unceasingly and diligently without the power henceforth to interfere in civil suits between parties, which we have expressly forbidden and prohibited; cognizance of these matters we are referring and assigning to our ordinary judges. ...

34 (b). FROM IBID., XIV, p. 209.
Ordinance of Moulins, February 1566, Art. 72.

As for those towns in which our officers ... and not the municipal councils and corporations have competence over police matters, we are resolved and hereby order that the *bourgeois* and citizens living

in each quarter or parish of these towns shall elect one or two of their
number to take charge and direction of police and everything involved
with it; and these *bourgeois* or citizens shall be eligible for election
irrespective of their quality and without any dispensations whatever.
They will have the authority to issue regulations and exercise dis-
training powers up to the value of sixty *sous* on any one occasion. At
the same time it will be possible to appeal against their ordinances and
acts of distraint; grievances will be readily heard and justice will be
given by the ordinary judges of the places concerned in assemblies of
the said *bourgeois* which will be held once a week before those judges
who, as indicated above, are responsible for police matters.

35. FROM C. LOYSEAU, *Cinq Livres du Droit des Offices avec le
Livre des Seigneuries et celui des Ordres,* chapter VII, 'Des Offices
des Villes', pp. 592–600.

... at Paris, La Rochelle, Dreux and in some other towns in France,
chiefly in the province of Picardy, there are town councils made up of
a certain number of permanent officers who are known as councillors
in some places, as peers in others, from amongst whom the aldermen
and principal town officials are normally chosen. . . . However, so that
they are not leaderless almost every town has a single principal officer
who . . . in France . . . is called the mayor . . . where there are only peers
or aldermen without a mayor the town's premier judge and chief
magistrate is empowered to preside and act as head of the aldermen,
in the capacity of a permanent mayor so that the town community
should not be without a leader . . . but then I have heard it said that
the lieutenant-general of Chartres has decreed that he should preside
not only over the citizens' general assemblies . . . but also over the
town council and private meetings of the aldermen. Indeed, it would
be very useful as a means of maintaining the citizens in a state of
complete obedience to the king if the king's chief official, representing
his Majesty, were to preside over town councils everywhere. Had that
been the situation before the recent disturbances it is probable that
they would not have taken place.

  In towns where there is a mayor or an equivalent head of the town
council, it is only right in every case that, having been elected by the
citizens, his appointment should subsequently be confirmed and
approved by the king. This is especially so in important towns whose
privileges his Majesty will always be more willing to maintain when
he knows that they are careful to choose officials who are acceptable
to him. In any event, it is indisputable that the mayor must be received
and sworn in by the king's chief judicial officer in the town. Likewise

it is a law common to the whole of France that in general assemblies of all the citizens of a town, it is not the mayor who presides but, in the absence of the governor, the lieutenant-general or another leading judicial officer who may be present. . . .

In some towns an ancient office still exists, that of *receveur des deniers communs* which by an edict of 1581 has been converted into a royal office. By this edict the king allowed the towns to put forward the names of three *bourgeois*, one of whom he would appoint to the office, in return for a money payment. Then, three or four years later, a royal declaration was promulgated, permitting the towns to reimburse these tax collectors and administer their funds through the municipal officials as had formerly been the practice. A number of towns took advantage of this offer.

From 1515 king Francis I established superintendants in the towns in order to supervise municipal officials and compel them to spend the towns' funds in accordance with royal ordinances. . . .

Municipal funds are generally called *deniers communs* in the same way as municipal matters are called *affaires communes*, because towns have corporative authority and a common purse. There are two sources from which towns may receive their money. In the first place there are patrimonial funds, which are the revenues drawn from estates and other endowments acquired by towns in any way other than by royal grant. Secondly, there are the funds obtained from certain levies conceded by the king which are raised each year in the towns and which may take the form of taxation reductions on corn or on wine, a concession over the price of salt, a toll on streams or crossings. Such funds are usually nominated in the original royal grant for a specific purpose; otherwise they have to be spent on fortification, on the upkeep of the streets, ramparts or gates of the town and may include the maintenance of the public clock, the cost of sentry-duty and of guarding the gates, but must not be diverted to any other use. As for the upkeep of the public fountains and the livelihood of preachers and schoolmasters only a maximum of one hundred *livres* per year may be spent on them. . . . But as for patrimonial funds they can be spent indiscriminately on any municipal requirements that the aldermen may ordain. It should also be noted that the accounts of the funds granted by the king must be laid before the *chambre des comptes*. Those of the patrimonial funds are laid before the bailiff or seneschal of the town; the *avocat* and *procureur du roi* are also summoned to attend and the mayor and aldermen must lend their assistance without payment or expenses . . . despite the frequency with which ancient French ordinances have declared royal officials incapable of holding municipal office, under pain of large fines, recent events have nevertheless demonstrated the value for the public of such an alliance and at present royal and municipal offices are frequently held together. . . .

36. FROM C. J. MAYER, *Des Etats-Généraux et autres Assemblées Nationales*, Paris, 1789, vol. IX, pp. 322 *et seq.*
Extracts from the *cahier* presented by the three estates in 1484.

. . . By a general edict [the king] should ordain that henceforth all the rights, liberties, exemptions, privileges and immunities of the Church, concerning both property and persons [*in rebus et personis*] will be faithfully and wholly observed and maintained, as was the case in the time of king Charles VII and his predecessors; and that the temporalty of clerics from this time forward will not be distrained nor subjected to embarrassment, except for a just and reasonable cause. . . .

Because the estate of nobility is indispensable to the defence, protection and safeguarding of the commonwealth, because it provides the kingdom's energy and vigour, it is absolutely necessary that noblemen, with their goods and estates, should continue to enjoy their exemptions, liberties, pre-eminences, rights, privileges, powers of jurisdiction and prerogatives in the same manner as they did in the time of king Charles VII and his predecessors and in keeping with royal ordinances concerning the privileges of the nobility. Because the nobility has been very much oppressed heretofore in a number of ways, and particularly by the frequency of the summoning of the *ban et arrière-ban* which has made it necessary for a number of them to sell their estates and hereditaments, being thereby reduced to great poverty, it is the opinion of the estates that in the future the *ban et arrière-ban* ought not to be summoned so frequently unless it is absolutely necessary for the defence and protection of the kingdom, and then only after careful deliberation in the council. And when noblemen are called out, they ought to be hired and paid fairly, each according to his position, so that they are not forced to live off the people. . . .

. . . the three estates wish to remonstrate further that though they appreciate that the position of the king and queen, the needs of the royal councillors and guards, the cost of embassies, the wages of royal officials, any other business which may arise, and also the upkeep of the army require the expenditure of money, nevertheless they are of the opinion that the revenue from the royal domain ought to be used first. When that source has proved inadequate, the people of France have always shown themselves ready and willing to assist the king by whatever means the members of the three estates meeting in formal session and duly apprised of the said lord [king's] affairs, have advised; such means are those least prejudicial to the people yet adequate to provide for the needs which arise. The people of France remain ready to help. Since the king has been pleased to offer to communicate all his business to us, here is the item of greatest importance about which the three estates most need to be acquainted: it concerns the amount of money necessary to maintain the items listed above, money levied in such a manner as to provide the most profit and the least harm, without the extortion and pillage which has been a feature of previous levies, and without its being used for purposes other than the welfare of the king and the preservation of the entire kingdom, Dauphiné and the areas bordering it. Therefore, the members of the three estates respectfully request the king to inform them on this matter.

If it should happen that the domain cannot provide the necessary amount and it becomes necessary to raise a subsidy outside it, the estates are of the opinion that the various impositions, salt taxes and equivalent raised in the past to provide for the war which was then being waged, amount to a lot more than the sum needed to maintain the above-listed items, without including the *tailles* at all; and they very much hope therefore that any reduction in the said impositions, salt taxes and equivalent, will be made impartially and reasonably, that the manner of their collection will be properly arranged and that there will be no levy of *tailles*.

Thus all the *tailles* and other equivalent taxes which have been in vogue in the past could be entirely removed and abolished; and henceforward, in keeping with the natural freedom of France and the doctrine of Saint Louis, who forbade his son to raise *tailles* from his people except in times of great emergency or want, no *tailles* nor equivalent subsidies should be imposed nor exacted without a prior assembly of the three estates, where the motives for taking such a step and the needs of the king and the kingdom would be made known and approval given by the estates without prejudice to the privileges of each part of the country. . . .

Item, the estates beg the king to confirm the liberties, privileges, exemptions, provisions and powers of jurisdiction of clerics, nobles, cities, the separate parts of the country and the towns of this kingdom, Dauphiné and the areas bordering it. . . .

37 (a). FROM IBID., vol. VII, p. 415.
Method of summoning the estates, 1576.

Wishing to assemble the estates in accordance with the ancient form, customarily observed in such convocations, the king issued express commissions as early as the month of August to all the bailiffs, seneschals, *prévôts*, judges, lieutenants, mayors and others concerned, requiring each of them, in their own area of jurisdiction, to convene clergymen, nobles and members of the third estate who had to consider amongst themselves the drawing up of *cahiers* and remonstrances and choose and elect from their number whomever they wished to take the said *cahiers* to the general assembly.

37 (b). FROM IBID., vol. XII, p. 344 *et seq.*

Letters of the king and queen to all provincial governors concerning the election of deputies to the Estates-General of 1614.

... having considered the advice of the queen regent, we have decided ... that the time is now appropriate to put into effect something which it has always been intended should take place at the king's coming of age, namely the meeting of a general assembly of the estates of all the provinces of this kingdom, where an account may be given of the events of our minority; where the present state of affairs may be set forth and provision made for the future by the establishment of a firm basis for the conduct of affairs and the administration of justice, police and finance; where counsel may be given on how best to provide relief for those subject to us and how best to redress those grievances and discords which, if slurred over, could prejudice our authority and the interests and welfare of all the orders of this kingdom....

For these reasons, we give you due notice that we intend to hold a meeting of the Estates-General comprising the freely appointed representatives of the three orders of our kingdom, which shall commence on the tenth day of September next, in our town of Sens, and there we expect and desire to find leading persons from each province, bailiwick and seneschalcy of this kingdom who will make known to us whatever remonstrances, complaints and grievances they may have, indicating also what means they would consider most suitable for settling the issues involved. Therefore we order and most strictly charge you immediately upon the receipt of this missive to have convened and assembled in the chief town of our jurisdictional area, within the shortest possible time, all those members of the three estates of that area who, according to custom and precedent, have to confer and communicate with one another regarding the remonstrances, complaints and grievances, and the arguments and opinions which should be put forward later at the Estates' general assembly; and who must then elect, choose and nominate from amongst themselves one representative of each order, men of ability and integrity whom they will send to our town of Sens ... with full instructions, sufficient documents and authority to enable them in accordance with the sound, ancient and commendable customs of this kingdom to inform us not only of their said remonstrances, complaints and grievances but also of how in their estimation the public good may best be safeguarded, our authority upheld, the ease and comfort of each and every individual assured; for our part, we affirm that they will find us ready and disposed to enforce the observance and full execution of whatever is decided upon . . .

38. FROM *ibid.*, vol. VII, pp. 334-5, Royal order for the convocation of the Estates-General in the town of Blois, 15 September, 1588.

. . . it is our will and intention that a meeting of the Estates-General, comprising the freely appointed representatives of the three orders of our kingdom, shall commence on the fifteenth day of August next, in our town of Blois, and there we expect to find leading persons from each province, bailiwick and seneschalcy who will make known to us in a plenary session the remonstrances, complaints and grievances of all the people, without constraint and without any insinuations which might favour the particular prejudices of individuals, whoever they may be. This meeting will provide a most appropriate and suitable means for obliterating and abolishing entirely the divisions presently existing between our subjects . . . and for reaching a safe and secure settlement by which our holy catholic religion will be completely re-stored and all heresy purged and extirpated from our kingdom, so that our subjects will no longer have any occasion to fear changes in religion, either during our lifetime or after our death. On all these matters and on any others which may be raised, offering the means to repair the corruption caused by the evils of war whether concern-ing the state of the Church, of the nobility and the third estate or affairs of justice, police and finance or contributing in general to the universal benefit of our kingdom, we intend to take apt and beneficial decisions . . .

39 (a). FROM *Bibliotheca Dumbensis ou Recueil de Chartres, Titres et Documents pour servir à l'histoire de Dombes*, ed. Valentin-Smith and C. Guigue, Trévoux, 1854–85, vol. I, LXXXI, pp. 431–2.

Official report of the taking over of Dombes, confiscated from the Constable de Bourbon, September 17, 1523.

. . . our lord the king has resolved and is resolved that all the lands of the said [Constable] de Bourbon shall be seized and taken under his control, as committed to and acquired by him ... the inhabitants have been informed that by way of provision and until such time as our lord the king ordains otherwise, they will be permitted and allowed to retain their former judicial privileges and their other prerogatives, liberties and exemptions; each and every one of them has taken an oath swearing to be, and in the future to remain, good and faithful subjects of our lord the king. ...

39 (b). FROM *Corps Universal Diplomatique du Droit des Gens,* ed. J. Du Mont, 8 vols., Amsterdam, 1726–39, VI, p. 272.
The Treaty of the Pyrenees, 1659.

It will also be within the power of his most Christian Majesty and at his discretion to prescribe to those inhabitants of the county of Roussillon who withdrew into Spain and whose return into the said county His Majesty will not find pleasing, the place in which they shall live, their appurtenances and their belongings: this without prejudice to any other liberties and privileges which have been granted to these people, which will be neither revoked nor altered.

40. FROM *Bibliotheca Dumbensis ou Recueil de Chartres, Titres et Documents pour servir à l'histoire de Dombes,* vol. I, LXXXI, pp. 470–1.
Henry II's request for a *don gratuit* of 10,000 *livres* in 1552 from the Estates of Dombes.

The king ... issued letters-patent addressed to his trusty and well-beloved Jean de Tignac, lieutenant-general of the seneschalcy of Lyons, instructing him to convene the estates of Dombes at Trévoux, to ask from them a free gift of 10,000 *livres* like the one which they had granted to his father, Francis I, in 1542. ... Monsieur de Tignac came to Trévoux on the fourteenth of June, having summoned the representatives of the three estates in the customary fashion. ... Monsieur de Tignac informed them of the king's intentions and of his need for funds and exhorted them to agree to the imposition of the 10,000 *livres* which the king was asking for. The deputies gave their opinions in the absence of Monsieur de Tignac. The Sire Varinier and the nobles were in favour of making the gift. Monsieur Nicole Melier replied for the third estate, arguing that in the past no more than two or three thousand *livres* had been granted and such grants had been delayed for two or three years; that 10,000 *livres* had never been granted and that the area was so poor that it would be difficult to find this amount in this year. He requested that the gift should be made in two payments, half in the current year and half in the following year. But after hearing Monsieur de Tignac's account of His Majesty's pressing needs it was agreed to pay the whole amount together. . . .

41. FROM *Documents Relatifs Aux Etats De Bretagne*, ed. C. de la Lande de Calan, Rennes, 1908, vol. I, pp. 194–5.
The Estates' reply to the royal commissioners in the meeting of 1568.

. . . we most humbly beg [the king] in keeping with his own promise and with that of his predecessors to maintain and preserve the honourable privileges, immunities, powers, prerogatives and liberties of the estates, which have been granted and conceded from time immemorial by the dukes and kings of glorious memory who have ruled over this land; and to respect and support the pacts, agreements, contracts and transactions solemnly entered into by them and the estates, serving both the king's interests and the needs and interests of the estates, without any diminution of ancient rights and duties . . . the obedience of his people cannot be more readily ensured . . . than by granting them the customary exemptions and liberties which they have always enjoyed . . . and it is certainly an act worthy of an excellent prince to allow his people to live according to their own worthy customs, their ancient and proper usages, which cannot be impaired or changed without the grave risk of harmful and dangerous consequences.

42 (a). FROM *Ordonnances Des Rois De France. Règne de François Ier*, Paris, 1902, vol. I, pp. 84–6, Royal letters of convocation to the Estates of Burgundy, February 6, 1515.

Francis, by the grace of God, king of France, to our trusty and well-beloved . . . subjects in the three estates of our land and duchy of Burgundy . . . having considered the advice of princes of the blood and of members of our *grand conseil*, we have written to instruct you to assemble in our town of Dijon on the twentieth of March next in order that the state of affairs may be explained to you and a request made to you on our behalf generously to grant and bestow on this occasion the sum of sixty thousand *livres*. . . .

42 (b). FROM *Documents Relatifs Aux Etats De Bretagne*, vol. I, pp. 109–10.
The Estates of 1542, official report.

After deliberation concerning the twenty thousand crowns asked for in addition to the seven *livres* hearth tax, the estates decided to present remonstrances to the Governor and to the other commissioners on the subject of the poverty of the people who, since the warrant and mandate expedited almost two years ago by the king authorizing the seizure of salt supplies, have had no means of raising money, for trade in salt remains forbidden to them as does all trade in connection with the sea from which they had been accustomed to collect the money to pay the hearth tax and the rents due to our lord; as a result, and with the added assistance of the hurricane which recently swept this land, they have become so needy that only with great difficulty could they pay the hearth tax required by the lord [king] and they could not find the means of supplying Monseigneur le Duc with the gift and donation of twenty thousand crowns unless they were first allowed freely to trade and bargain for salt as they had done before the above-mentioned warrant was issued, and unless the *gabelle* was removed, all of which they entreat should be done. On condition that the *gabelle* is removed and they are permitted to trade and bargain for salt as they did before the despatch of the said warrant, and not otherwise, they will consent to the gift of twenty thousand crowns. This levy must not take the form of a hearth tax, nor may it be established as a precedent for the future; nor may the collectors take any dues from the collection. Otherwise the gift will not be granted, for the tax-payers are so poor that it is quite plain that they ought not to bear it.

42 (c). FROM *Cahiers des Etats de Normandie*, pp. 173–4.
Estates of September 1633; Extract from the register of the *greffier-commis* of the Estates.

Consideration was given to a *lettre de cachet* from his Majesty issued at Mouceaux on the seventh of this month, signed 'Louis' and countersigned 'Phélypeaux' and addressed to the deputies, in which his Majesty expressed the wish that Monsieur de la Mailleraye, the king's lieutenant-general in this province, should, like his predecessor, the Sire de Villars, be granted the sum of 6,000 *livres*. The letter was read and a majority of the deputies, who had been assembled through the bailiwicks, were in favour of granting the sum of 6,000 *livres* to the said Monseigneur de la Mailleraye, but for this year only and on condition that no inferences should be drawn for the future.

43. FROM D. J. BUISSERET, *Annales de Normandie*, XIII, 1963, 'Lettres Inédites de Sully aux Trésoriers Généraux de France à Caen (1599–1610)', no. 40, p. 299.

Sirs,

If I have delayed until now to write to you about the wretched misfortune which has afflicted this kingdom, the excess of my grief must
serve as my excuse. Truly this great calamity has been more percept-
ible to me than to any other, who has seen his country lose a good
king who had raised it to the height of felicity and who has himself
lost a good master who loved me and whom I honoured to a degree
beyond all earthly comprehension. Besides this matter, I have also been
forced to keep silent because of the continual tasks which we have had
to undertake up to now to settle the principal affairs of this state. . . . I
desire by this letter . . . that you do not fail in the performance of your
obligations and in the exercise of your offices according to the regulations and with the care which your own consciences dictate. The king
and the queen regent, his mother, with the advice of the princes,
prelates and other leading officers of this kingdom, have resolved that
financial matters shall be conducted in the future in the accustomed
manner and form and they have charged me to administer them as I
did under the late king, as you may be informed in letters from their
Majesties. Without your help in the provinces it would be difficult
for me to carry out my responsibilities, as I could wish and I believe
that over and above your general sense of duty, you will be willing to
make an additional gesture of diligence on my behalf; that being so,
I entreat you henceforth to redouble your efforts in the work of your
office and to assist me in carrying out mine. Among other matters,
be prompt in handing over the king's revenue into the hands of the
central treasurer [trésorier de l'épargne], not only the receipts for
the last quarter but for future ones too, as they fall due, taking
care nevertheless that the people with whose preservation their
Majesties are particularly concerned, are in no way subjected to
oppression. Because the central treasurer will write to you more fully
about the state of his business with your collector-general, I will only
add on this occasion that I promise to inform their Majesties of
your faithful service so that they may be grateful for it. As for me,
I will always bear it in mind in order that I may have your support
when it is needed and so that I may convey to you, sirs, that I am your
most affectionate friend and servant.
          [signed]   le duc de Sully.
Paris, this May 30, 1610.

44. FROM O. RANUM, *Richelieu and the Councillors of Louis XIII*,
pp. 109–10, July 1635, Abel Servien (secretary of state) to Claude
le Bouthillier (superintendent of finance, acting in the capacity
of secretary of state).

I have been ordered to tell you that the king wishes you to write in his name to the provincial governors, or in their absence, to the lieutenant generals of your department, that they are to send His Majesty as soon as possible a list of those who have come to them and are prepared to serve in the *arrière-ban;* and that they [the governors] are to order the bailiffs and other judges very explicitly to take proceedings against defaulters by seizure of their fiefs and by other customary means in accordance with the severity of the ordinances.

45. FROM RAYMOND DE BECCARIE DE PAVIE, SIEUR DE FOURQUEVAUX, *Instructions sur le Faict de la Guerre,* ed. G. Dickinson, London, 1954, Book I, pp. 5 *et seq.*

[Louis XI] was the first king of France to begin to employ foreigners, the Swiss in particular: he normally kept six thousand of them on hire. Charles VIII followed that precedent and led a large force of Swiss troops into Naples. Louis XII also employed them a great deal, as well as Germans and other foreigners. The king who occupies the throne at present has acted likewise in all the wars in which he has been engaged. It has at last been realized, however, that Frenchmen can serve the king as well as foreigners, that they are inured to the hardships of war.... Accordingly, so I believe, large numbers of legionaries have been raised in this kingdom....

Nations which have been concerned in the past with the disposition of infantry have raised variously styled detachments though all roughly equal numerically, consisting of between six and eight thousand men. The Romans called them legions, the Greeks phalanxes, the French troupes and nowadays the Swiss and Germans have a name for them in their own language which is equivalent to 'battalion' in ours; the Italians and Spaniards use the same word but ... because the king has preferred to use the term [legion] as more fitting I will do so likewise. Because the Roman legion was composed of six thousand men, ours will have that number also, but whereas theirs was divided into ten battalions ours will contain twelve, the additional two being the *enfants perdus,* those troops who must engage the enemy first. Each of the ten battalions will be commanded by a captain and under each captain there will be a lieutenant, a standard bearer, a sergeant, an officer in charge of military discipline, a quarter-master, two drums and a fife; and in addition to all these, each captain will have under his command five hundred and ten men, divided into six small companies which will be commanded by six corporals or centurians. Five of the companies will be reserved for the main body of the battalion and the sixth for the flank. Under each corporal there will be four platoon commanders [*caps d'esquadre*], under each platoon commander two *dizeniers* or section commanders [*chefs de chambre*] and under each section commander there will be nine men. Thus the platoon commander will be in charge of twenty men, and he will be the twenty-first. The corporal will be in charge of eighty-five men, himself included. Four of these corporals will have companies composed entirely of pikemen, a fifth will be made up almost entirely of halberdiers, but because of the need to strengthen the halberdiers' flanks, each section of this particular company must include three pikemen, the remainder being halberdiers. The sixth company shall be made up half of pikemen and half of musketeers. . . . The two companies of *enfants perdus* will total 868 men, 434 in each company. Each of them will have a captain in command who will have the same number of officers and men with special duties as the other ten captains. And the remaining 425 will be divided into five small companies under the command of five corporals, and each corporal will have under him as many platoons and men as one of the other ten corporals mentioned above. Four of these companies will be composed of musketeers mixed with a number of bowmen. The fifth will be composed entirely of pikemen, and called the *extraordinaires,* since they fight out of order and without maintaining their line. The total number of men in all these companies added together, comes to six thousand and seventy, and besides these, each legion must have an overall commander above the captains, who will be a colonel and who will have the following officers: a camp-master, a serjeant-major, a provost. The provost will have under his command a number of able men to assist him in reaching his verdicts and to provide forensic advice; he will also have a clerk and some serjeants or constables [*archers*] . . . the colonel-general will also have a priest or two to conduct divine service and to administer the sacraments of the Church to the members of the Legion. There must also be a doctor, an apothecary and a surgeon, also somebody to make fireworks and gunpowder and a gunsmith. . . .

. . . the mistake made today in our *compagnies d'ordonnance* is that young men are made men-at-arms as soon as they cease to be pages or leave school. In order to improve our companies it would be necessary to draw up an ordinance forcing all young men who want to become members of mounted companies, upon reaching the age of seventeen, with the exception only of princes, to become musketeers [*arquebusiers*] for two or three years and then light horsemen [*estradiots*] for a similar time and then light cavalrymen, in which three conditions of soldiering they would learn all that was necessary for a good horseman to know. In the course of this apprenticeship they would outgrow the fury and fire of youth, becoming dispassionate and reasonable so that they could exercise command judiciously among the men-at-arms, of whose number they would have to remain for three or four years. When that period had passed, if they remained men-at-arms by reason of possessing a fief, they would be bound to leave their *compagnies d'ordonnance* and return to their homes, there to remain ready for service whenever the command might come. This rule should be maintained for all those liable for service, whatever their age. Otherwise the duty of *arrière-ban* which French noblemen owe to the king will be destroyed. Even at present it has lost much of its force. The reason for this is that everybody wishes to be a member of a mounted company, gaining exemption thereby from the *arrière-ban,* so that the governor who ought to raise five or six hundred men-at-arms could not at present raise even one hundred, however much he tried, and those who responded would be so badly equipped that the sight of them would be derisory. And this profession [of arms] is further disparaged by those who do not belong to *compagnies d'ordonnance* but who seek exemption by sending some squire in their place, to an assembly which formerly all the great men of France considered it a great honour to attend in person.

46. FROM *Lettres De Henri III, Roi de France*, vol. II, pp. 224–6, 1429, To the *seigneur* de Mandelot, Paris, September 4, 1575.

Monsieur de Mandelot.[1] My cousin, the Cardinal of Armagnac, foreseeing from the enemy's actions that he is not inclined to seek a settlement and that only force will persuade him to make peace, has proposed that I should draw up an army of three thousand men and five or six hundred cavalry with the necessary provisions, at the common expense of my lands of Dauphiné, Provence and the County of Avignon; he has offered to contribute a thousand infantrymen and their pay, as well as whatever cavalry he can manage, and his share of the provisions. With this force we could try to retake little by little the places under occupation, thereby robbing the enemy of their ability to act as aggressors because of the lack of unity and harmony between these provinces. I approve the suggestion and have sent off a despatch to the *sires* de Gordes and de Carces so that they may join up with my cousin to bring the enterprise to a satisfactory conclusion. Before concluding this despatch I must add that I have received news, confirmed from a number of sources, of the arrival of the son of the late Admiral, with some followers, in the valley of Quyras in Dauphiné and he has been joined by small bands from Geneva as well as the leading members of that faction and all the forces which they can

---

[1] Mandelot was governor at Lyons, 1568-81.

gather together. This has not only reinforced my desire for the above-mentioned union to take place—and I am now writing to urge it with all speed—but it has also persuaded me of the need for further reinforcements. Therefore I have thought to use your company and that of the *seigneur* of La Barge with the two ensigncies of infantry which you have and the regiment of Count Martinenge which I believe is at present in Vivaretz, in order to make the *sire* de Gordes so strong that he can hinder the enemy's plans and bring them to battle if the occasion presents itself. If they fall upon Provence I will send him word to hand over all his forces to the *sire* de Carces; meanwhile I request you, Monsieur de Mandelot, as soon as you know where and when the union of our forces is to take place, to see that those soldiers under your orders are sent to join the rest, their expenses being borne by people within your *gouvernement* for as long as they are forced to remain there, so that by a neighbourly effort we may put a stop to the evil which menaces all to an equal extent ... I have also written to my cousin, the *duc* d'Uzès that if Marshal Dampville seems ready to cross the Rhône to seek allies he must forthwith send Colonel Staupitz with his regiment of cavalry [*reistres*] to *sire* de Gordes and, as soon as he can, forestall and overtake the Marshal. ...

P.S. Monsieur de Mandelot, insofar as the main point of the war may fall in your *gouvernement,* I beg you to keep a constant watch over everything relating to my service and the maintenance of the forces which must be assembled there, including the stores, to avoid the possibility of any disorder. I am instructing the companies of my uncle, the Duke of Savoy, of the Prince of Piedmont and of the Viscount of La Guierche to hold themselves ready to come to Lyons as soon as I give the word, as well as yours and those of the *sire* de Suzes, the count de Bennes, the *sires* Maugiron and La Barge which I believe are already in the field. ...

47 (a) FROM *Recueil Des Lois,* XIV, p. 439.
Ordinance of Blois, 1579, Articles 260–1.

We have forbidden the captains of our bodyguard to admit on to the muster roles of their companies anyone who is not a nobleman, a captain or a distinguished soldier, nor may their offices be sold directly nor indirectly.

Nobody can be admitted to a position in our household guards if he has not previously spent three full years in one of our *compagnies d'ordonnance* or has served as a captain in command of infantry.

I

47 (b). ISAMBERT, vol. XVI, pp. 284–5.
Code Michaud, 1629, Articles 225–9.

With regard to our troops, both cavalry and infantry, their administration and their discipline, the civil wars have been responsible for the disorderly conduct which most of them are displaying at present; and the extent of the harm caused by their licentious behaviour is not adequately provided for in the ancient military ordinances. We have judged it fitting, therefore, for the well-being of our state, the good conduct of our troops and the relief of our people to make the necessary provisions in a new regulation, without detracting from precedents which are not contrary to this new regulation; consequently, we have enacted, decreed and ordained, and enact, decree and ordain ... that the salary of captains and officers will be increased by half, that is to say:

For staff-officers, per month,

A camp-master, 500 *livres,* a sergeant-major, 300 *livres,* an adjutant, 100 *livres,* a provost, his officers and constables, 360 *livres,* a sergeant-major of cavalry, 60 *livres,* a chaplain, 30 *livres,* a surgeon, 30 *livres.* ...

For a company of 200 men,

A captain, 300 *livres,* a lieutenant, 100 *livres,* an ensign, 73 *livres,* each of two sergeants, 30 *livres,* each of three corporals, 20 *livres,* each of six lance-corporals (*anspesades*), 17 *livres* ... each of thirty-seven cadets, 10 *livres,* each of two drummers, 15 *livres,* a surgeon, 15 *livres,* a quarter-master, 15 *livres.* ...

As to those soldiers who distinguish themselves by the quality of their service, they will receive an increase in their pay on the testimonial of a general, a brigadier (*maréchal-de-camp*), a camp-master and a captain, but not otherwise.

By means of their service, soldiers may attain places and offices in companies, passing from rank to rank to the grade of captain and even higher if they prove themselves worthy.

48. FROM *Lettres De Henri III, Roi De France,* vol. II, pp. 73–5, 1160, To the Seigneur de Rambouillet, Avignon, November 29, 1574.

Monsieur de Rambouillet.[1] Upon my arrival in this kingdom I declared and made known in two letters-patent my singular desire and intention to look to the tranquillity of my kingdom and the security and preservation of all my subjects who have been or still may be of the new party [huguenots] when they behave as they should; in so doing, I would have thought that I had thereby provided at least the chief and prin-

[1] Rambouillet was lieutenant-general of Maine.

cipal remedies and prerequisites for bringing about a settlement of the war and divisions which currently disunite my subjects. Nevertheless, although those who have revolted ought to renounce their evil undertaking and give me the obedience they owe, on the contrary they have urged others who are peacefully residing in their houses, and are still urging them, to act like them and thus strengthen their party, and to this end they have circulated a number of false rumours, succeeding thereby—so I have heard—in stirring some of the most docile into revolt and the taking up of arms, as the continual meetings, comings and goings between each other's houses, the marches of armed bands by night and the sale of their produce and personal property, demonstrate well enough. To deal with this situation, I have decided to write this letter to tell you that in accordance with my honest and sincere intention, stated in my letters, I wish you to continue to assure all those who have been or may still be of the new party and who remain in their homes, and others who may be in a state of fear and distrust, that I have no other wish than to maintain and preserve the security of their lives and possessions so long as they remain quietly in their houses without undertaking anything contrary to the good of my service, in accordance with the contents of my above-mentioned letters-patent which I desire to be inviolably kept and observed. But if you discover. . . anybody seeking to act in a manner prejudicial to my service, it is my wish that before they have time to do so, especially those who move by night and with arms, whose intentions must be mischievous, you should fall upon them as rebels in so far as my power and authority enables you to do so. I desire further that in order to lighten the burden on my subjects and relieve them from the great oppressions and exactions inflicted upon them by the soldiers in my service as they move from one province or garrison to another, you should see to the exact observance of the ordinance . . . which stipulates that my soldiers shall not pass from one *gouvernement* to another without being accompanied by commissioners who will be provided by the governor or lieutenant-general of the province whence they are departing; the latter will warn the governor or lieutenant-general of the province whither they are proceeding and he will send a commissioner ahead to meet them, accompany them and see that they behave in an orderly fashion *en route.* . . .

(ii). The King's Men

49. FROM O. RANUM, *Richelieu and the Councillors of Louis XIII*, pp. 189–91, Regulations drawn up by the king concerning the role of the secretary of state for war and the authority of the other secretaries of state.

The king wills and ordains that the secretary for war shall be responsible to his Majesty for commissioning, mustering and making all other necessary provisions for the chief and principal army which must be commanded by his Majesty or by his lieutenant-general. But if besides this principal army there is a need to raise more forces or one or more armies in the provinces, the secretary in charge of the area from which they are to be raised shall be responsible for their commissioning and mustering and for making all the other provisions which may subsequently be necessary. . . . And if it should happen that the armies have been raised to serve in a number of provinces cutting across departmental responsibilities, the secretaries concerned shall agree amongst themselves as to which of them shall take responsibility or alternatively responsibility shall devolve upon the secretary whose department covers the greatest part of the provinces concerned. The districts and meeting places in which new troops are to be raised will be nominated, as is customary, by the marshals of France, and official correspondence on this matter which goes to governors of the provinces and towns and to the inhabitants of these areas will be signed by the secretary in charge of the department in which these places are situated, whilst that concerning the superintendence of the troops addressed to commanders and commissioners will be signed by the secretary for war; after the said troops have joined the main body of the army for which they were intended, responsibility will rest with whoever is in command of that army.

In order that his Majesty may be informed of the state of the various garrisons, the secretaries will be summoned to a joint meeting with the king so that each can give his opinion about what needs to be done in the provinces under his jurisdiction and report the changes which have been made in the course of the year. His Majesty can then decide upon the appropriate estimates and the number of soldiers who will be needed in each of the garrisons. At the same time, the secretary for war shall draw up a general estimate in accordance with his Majesty's instructions, the accounts for which will have to be settled in the usual chamber [the *Chambre des Comptes*] whilst the individual lists will be despatched by the secretaries concerned to the governors and captains of the various places and these secretaries will be responsible, each in his own area, for all the procedures necessary to implement the individual estimates in regard to each of the above mentioned governors. If his Majesty judges it necessary and therefore commands that some change should be made in the garrisons in the course of the year, whether to transfer them from one place to another or to increase or diminish their number, the changes will be made on the authority of the secretaries in the areas concerned who will inform the secretary for war.

All official communications on the subject of the raising of infantry and cavalry to serve on campaign under the command of colonels of infantry and light cavalry, will be the responsibility of the secretary for war. As for the raising and commissiong of other soldiers for service in fortified places and garrisons the other secretaries, each in his department, shall be responsible and will communicate with the governors, captains, mayors and aldermen of the towns to organize the billetting of the troops.

The general estimate for the artillery will be made by the secretary for war like those involving the royal army for which he is properly responsible, but should any matter arise which concerns the shifting, casting, remounting or addition of cannon, or the making of powder and shot for the security and defence of these fortified places, then responsibility will fall to the secretary for the relevant area.

The provision of the titles and offices of Constable, grandmaster of artillery and colonel of infantry will appertain to the secretary for war and the other offices of the crown or the royal household to the other secretaries who are accustomed to perform this function as part of their departmental duties, while the office of marshal of France will be provided by the secretary whose turn it is to sit in the council when the king issues the appropriate order.[1]

The secretary in charge of the royal household will deal with despatches on the subject of the members of the royal bodyguard. . . .
                    [signed]   Louis
Given at Saint Germain-en-Laye, on April 29, 1619, by royal order.

50. FROM *Correspondance de la Mairie de Dijon,* ed. J. Garnier, Dijon, 1870, vol. III, p. 257.

By order of the king. To our dear and well-beloved subjects: Having ordered the sire du Chastelet, a councillor in our *Conseil d'Etat* and a *maître des requêtes* attached to our household, to return to our province of Burgundy to deal with any matters of importance concern-

---

[1] Besides being full members of the administrative councils, the secretaries also attended the *conseil d'en haut* on a rota system to keep the king and his advisers informed of what took place at the other council meetings.

ing our administration in that province, we have also decided to entrust him with this letter for you, by which we command and order you to give complete credence to whatever he says about our intentions in these matters and, so that he may expedite our orders, we require you to give all the help that he may ask of you. Such is our will; and we expect to be obeyed.

Given at Sens, the 18 March, 1631.

[signed]   Louis

[counter-

signed]   Phélypeaux

To our dear and well-beloved mayor and aldermen in our town of Dijon.

51 (a). FROM D. J. BUISSERET, Annales de Normandie, XIII, 'Lettres Inédites de Sully aux Trésoriers Généraux de France à Caen (1599–1610), No. 11, p. 278.

Sirs,

You received several letters from me some days ago in which I replied fully to your earlier correspondence. This present communication is simply to accompany the estimate and warrant authorizing the raising of a subvention in your *généralité* to replace the one *sou* per *livre* tax which has been neither fixed nor farmed at its true worth. You will apply yourselves carefully to the task of collecting the amount set down in the estimate so that his Majesty may be sure to receive what has been promised and no less than the original estimate of what was due from the tax of one *sou* per *livre*. Your task is to have the warrant put into effect without handing it over to the bailiffs or to anybody else; that is not necessary since the tax is being replaced by a straightforward subvention. Confident that you will treat this matter with the attention and responsibility expected of you, I will say no more about it, asking God to preserve you, Sirs, in his safekeeping. Given at Fontainebleau, on the thirtieth day of April, 1600.

51 (b). FROM IBID., No. 18, pp. 283–4.

Sirs,

Having been warned at the time of our decision to regulate the currency[1] that the rumour was widespread that the king intended, by raising the value of money, to make a profit for himself at his people's

---

[1] By the edict of Monceaux, September, 1602.

expense, we were anxious to make it clear that his intention was quite the contrary and that the rumour was completely unfounded; we therefore thought of having warrants despatched to all the *généralités*, like the one that I recently sent to you, to provide a means, if possible, for the people to profit from the increased value of the money which they would pay into the hands of the collectors and tax-gatherers. Since then, however, I have received the opinions and remonstrances conveyed to me by your colleagues in some of the *généralités* to the effect that it is quite impossible to implement this warrant in full, chiefly in respect of the arrangements between the tax-gatherers and the tax-payers, which would so increase costs and the number of legal suits as to outweigh the increase in the value of the currency. All these considerations have been laid before the council and we have decided to follow the advice given to us by your confrères, namely no longer to concern ourselves with making deductions for individual tax-payers but only to instruct our tax-gatherers, collectors and collector-general (*récéveur-général*) to keep accounts, and later the king might well decide to remit to the people of each *généralité* a sum proportionate to the profit received by his Majesty, which would go some way towards meeting the loss.

Given at Paris on the eighteenth day of October, 1602

Your most affectionate friend and servant,

[signed]   Rosny[2]

Sirs, I beg you to send me without delay a list and memorial of the towns in your *généralité* which are exempt from payment of the *tailles,* together with those owing a stated amount which will nevertheless be distinguished from the remainder.

52. FROM E. PASQUIER, *Les Recherches de la France*, Paris, 1596, p. 82.

... formerly our kings recompensed their captains and brave soldiers with noble fiefs, but with the passage of time this source of bounty dried up (because the whole kingdom had been distributed) and they were forced to consider an alternative form of recompense, not in reality as rich and opulent as the granting of fiefs, but offering greater honour. As a result of royal ingenuity, or perhaps through the wisdom of royal counsellors, the order of knighthood was elaborated. Where previously kings had rewarded their subjects with land and possessions, as they acquired more provinces they began instead to acknowledge good and faithful service in a more personal way, with an embrace.

[2] He only became Duke of Sully in March, 1606; until then he signed himself as *Marquis* of Rosny.

These embraces became a religious ceremony. When the king wished to inspire a group of noblemen or gallant soldiers to fight well in battle or to thank them at the conclusion of some undertaking, he embraced them. In so doing, and with little ceremony, he bestowed knighthoods upon them. . . . This order was originally invented, as the derivation of the word *chevalier* suggests, for the benefit of those who followed the profession of arms. However, as more time elapsed, members of the legal profession began to seek knighthoods to go with their honours and offices. As a result two sorts of knight appeared: knights of arms and knights of the law. . . . Thus Froissart in chapter one hundred and seventy seven of the first book of his *Histoires* tells of three knights, two of whom professed arms and the third the law.

53. FROM D. J. BUISSERET, *Annales de Normandie*, XIII, 'Lettres Inédites de Sully aux Trésoriers Généraux de France à Caen (1599–1610)', No. 12, pp. 278–9.

Sirs,

As soon as I received your letter with the accompanying decree from the *Cour des Aides* at Rouen verifying the continuance of the new impositions, I decided that it was right to have all the restrictions included in the said decree lifted in order to avoid the possibility of a reduced income. For this purpose I have despatched a *lettre de jussion*[1] to the court in which I have written in some detail on this subject. I consider that they will take notice of my order and give satisfaction in a matter which they believe, as we do, concerns his Majesty's service. Meanwhile you have done well to begin early the task of publicising the sale of contracts for the farming of these impositions for I hope that before time grows short we shall have what we want from the said court [*des Aides*]. Then you will be able to proceed directly with the contracts according to the warrant which I am sending with this letter, without any ensuing reduction of revenue; I am not convinced that the impositions levied in your *généralité* should raise as little as you have hitherto indicated, without bad husbandry; for the income amounts to barely a quarter of the sum raised in the *généralité* of Rouen whereas it ought to be a third. I beg you to scrutinize this matter and to take great care in renewing the recent contracts, about which you will give me an account, as about the other matters in your care. . . .

Given at Moulins, on the twenty-sixth day of June, 1600.

[1] Orders sent to a sovereign count demanding immediate and unqualified registration of royal legislation.

54. FROM F. AUBERT, *Histoire du Parlement de Paris de l'Origine à François Ier*, Paris, 1894, vol. I, pp. 381–3, Appendix XII.
Extracts from the *Parlement's* registers on the drawing up of customs.

11 February, 1501. This day the court, having listened to the *procureur-général*, has ordained and ordains that the customs of the Duchy of Bourbonnais lately written down and published in that locality by the king's command, together with the official report of *maître* Thibault Baillet, a royal councillor and president and Guillaume de Besançon, a royal councillor in the court, who were entrusted with this task by the sovereign, will be sent to the said court's registry. . . .

13 November, 1509. This day after *maître* Thibault Baillet, a president in this court had placed before it the customs of the locality of Maine, which he and *maître* Jehan le Lievre, a royal councillor in the court, have published by the express orders of the sovereign in the town of Le Mans, together with their official report, the court has ordained and ordains that parties to a legal suit, needing to examine any of the customs granted and published, will be given the relevant extract signed by the chief clerk of the court.

15 January, 1510. This day the court has ordained and ordains that the customs of the bailiwick of Amiens, which have been delivered to the registry of this court by the commissioners and which are only signed by *maître* Guillaume de Besançon, a royal councillor in this court, one of ten commissioners, including the late *maître* Christophe de Carmanne, a former councillor and president in this court who did not sign them, will be collated with the similar customs signed by the above-mentioned ten commissioners, which were handed over to the lieutenant of the bailiff of Amiens. By order of this court, these customs have been sent on here and will be signed by the chief clerk of this court.

55. FROM *Les Edits Et Ordonnances Des Rois De France,* ed. A Fontanon, Paris, 1611, vol. II, pp. 576–7.
The Paulette, December 1604.

Henry, by the grace of God, king of France and Navarre, etc. Having never desired anything more than the opportunity to indicate to our subjects in general and to our officers in particular the effects of our favour we have recently listened with a good deal of satisfaction to the supplications and remonstrances which have been made to us by a number of the chief and most senior officers of this kingdom seeking to persuade us to introduce some regulation into the practice of resignation of office so that they should not be forced, when they are elderly and consequently more capable of exercising them worthily, to resign their offices in favour of younger and less experienced men in order to avoid the loss of such a large sum as the value of their offices entails: consequently, recognizing the considerable interest of our officers, the good which we will do in this kingdom by keeping offices in the hands of those most skilled in affairs and their readiness to pay the four *deniers per livre*[1] tax on the estimated value of their offices which we will collect annually from those who are prepared to raise the said tax in order to redeem themselves from the severity of the forty day rule,

For all these reasons after having deliberated over this matter in our council, in which were a number of princes of the royal blood, officers of our crown and other *seigneurs* and notable personages who have judged this proposal just and advantageous to our officers and worthy of the affection that we have for our subjects; with their advice and in conformity with the decree already issued on this matter, and with our certain knowledge, full power and royal authority we have by this present declaration ... decreed and declared ... that henceforward, the officers of our kingdom, whether judicial, financial or of any other kind, whatever their station ... who are subject to the forty day rule ... shall be dispensed from the rigour of the forty days which each of these officers must survive after his resignation, counting from the day and date of the receipt of money paid into the *Parties Casuelles*,[2] by the annual payment of four *deniers per livre* of the estimated value of their offices by those who wish voluntarily to avail themselves of this favour and dispensation ... in return for this money, if they should die during the year, their offices will not be declared vacant and obtainable for our profit, but will be kept in favour of their resignees as far as those offices which are subject to suppression are concerned; and as for those which are not subject to suppression, they will go to the widows and heirs who may dispose of them as they see fit and to their own profit, as something belonging to them; ... all officers who will have paid the said tax shall enjoy the said favour and dispensation during the year for which they have paid, their guarantee being simply the receipt for the money contributed for the said annual right of dispensation duly signed by *maître* Charles Paulet, a secretary of our chamber. ...

---

[1] Equal to one sixtieth.
[2] The treasurer of the *Parties Casuelles* was responsible for the money gathered for the royal exchequer from the sale of office.

56 (a). FROM J. F. BLUCHE, *L'Origine des Magistrats du Parlement de Paris*, Paris, 1956.

The Chevalier Family:

I   Georges Ier Ch., graduate in laws, living at Rheims in 1523, given the title of esquire in 1520. He was then *enquêteur* for the king in the bailiwick of Vermandois. He married Jeanne Beguin, daughter of a merchant *bourgeois* of Rheims.

II   Georges II Ch., titled esquire in the marriage contract of his son, Claude, graduate in laws, councillor in the *présidial* court of Rheims. . . .

III   Claude Ch., (died 1627), esquire, *seigneur* of La Glasolle, St-Hilaire and Moivre, councillor in the *présidial* court and lieutenant-general of the bailiwick of Rheims in 1580; he married in 1577 Marguerite Godet, daughter of Guillaume, *seigneur* of St-Hilaire and Moivre, collector-general of the *taillon* in Champagne.

IV   Nicolas Ch., esquire, *seigneur* of Le Boschet, collector of *tailles* at Nogent-sur-Seine. . . .

V   Louis Ier Ch., (Nogent, 1640-died 1715), *seigneur* of St-Hilaire, Moivre, etc., councillor in the *présidial* court at Sedan of which he was also dean, treasurer of France, intendant of *gabelles* and domain . . . farmer-general from 1695 to 1715, private secretary to the king from 1701 until his death. He married in 1667 Marguerite Estienne, daughter of Philbert, *seigneur* of Augny, lieutenant-general in the bailiwick of Metz.

56 (b). The Phélypeaux Family:

III   Guillaume le Picart, called Phélypeaux (died 1509), *bourgeois* of Blois, *seigneur* of Ville-Sablon. . . .

IV   Raymond Ier Phélypeaux (died 1553). . . .

V   Louis Ph., *seigneur* of La Cave and La Vrillière, councillor in the *présidial* court at Blois. . . .

VI   Raymond II Ph., (Blois 1560-Suze 1629), esquire, *seigneur* of Herbault and La Vrillière, central treasurer [*trésorier de l'Epargne*], councillor of state, secretary of state in 1621 after having been a private secretary to the king from 1590 to 1619. . . .

VII   Balthazar Ph. (died 1663), knight, *seigneur* of Herbault, councillor in the *parlement* [of Paris] (1618), central treasurer, councillor of state. . . .

56 (c). The Turgot Family:

I   Jean T., *seigneur* of Les Tourailles, declared non-noble in 1463, confirmed as a nobleman in 1473 by virtue of a charter granted by Louis XI on 5 November 1470; married Phélipe Bertrand, daughter of Gilles, *seigneur* of Les Tourailles.

II   Pierre T. (died 1508), esquire, *seigneur* of La Bellaize and of Les Tourailles....

III Guille T. (died 1541), *seigneur* of Les Tourailles and of La Selle, etc., married in 1508, Jehanne Le Verrier, daughter of Jehan, knight, baron of Vassy.

IV   Loys T. (died about 1588), *seigneur* of Les Tourailles and of La Thrésorée, councillor in the *présidial* court at Caen, *maître des requêtes* for the *duc* d'Alençon (1568)....

V   Antoine Ier T. (died 1616), *seigneur* of La Restaudière, St-Clair, etc., barrister in the *parlement* of Rouen....

VI   Jacques T. (died in Paris, 1659), *seigneur* of St-Clair, councillor in the *parlement* of Rouen (1616), *intendant* of Normandy, Picardy and then Berry, councillor of state (1643)....

VII Antoine II T. (1625-Paris, 1713), *seigneur* of St-Clair, knight of the Order of Malta, councillor in the *parlement* of Paris (1660), *maître des requêtes* (1667), *intendant* of Limoges (1671), married in 1668 Jeanne Marie du Tillet de la Bussière, daughter of a president in the chamber of *requêtes* [in the *parlement* of Paris].

57. FROM *Ducuments Relatifs à L'Administration Financière en France de Charles VII à François Ier* (1443–1523), ed. G. Jacqueton, Paris, 1891, pp. 205 *et seq., Le Vestige des Finances.*

Question: In what do the finances of the kingdom consist?

Answer: There are two kinds of finances, ordinary and extraordinary.

Q: What are ordinary finances?

A: These appertain to the king's domain and are governed and administered by the four treasurers of France, one each in charge of Languedoil, Outre-Seine, Normandy and Languedoc.

Q: How are these funds collected?

A: The normal collectors from the bailiwicks, seneschalcies and viscounties are chiefly responsible, under the above-mentioned treasurers of France....

Q: What are extraordinary finances?

A: These are revenues from the *greniers,* the *aides* and *tailles* of the kingdom....

Q: What is the function of an officer in charge of a *grenier*?

A: A *grenetier* must collect the salt tax which is owed to the king on salt sold and distributed at the *grenier*....

Receipts from the *aides*, a 5% or 12½% tax on wine, varying according to local custom, are allotted to tax-farmers who are appointed annually by the *élus* and their clerks in the various *élections*. . . .

The collector of *tailles* receives from the tax-gatherers of each parish or village in the *élection* the amount assessed by the *élu* who has been ordered and commissioned to raise a certain sum as the contribution of his *élection* to the total *taille* to be levied on the whole kingdom. . . .

58. FROM IBID., June 1500. Edict on the jurisdiction of the *Cour des Aides*, the *élus* and the *grenetiers*.

Louis, by the grace of God, king of France, to all those who will see these letters, greetings. From the time when the *aides*, *tailles* and *gabelles* were first imposed in this kingdom to raise money for the defence and protection of the subjects and of the body politic, our royal predecessors appointed and established in the dioceses, towns and other areas of the kingdom *élus* in the case of *aides* and *tailles*, and *grenetiers* and superintendants in the case of the *gabelles*, who had competence in the first instance to examine and determine all civil and criminal cases arising out of these matters, which on appeal were dealt with by the sovereign court established for that purpose; subsequently our more recent predecessors . . . have on many different occasions willed, ordained and proclaimed by irrevocable edicts and ordinances that competence and jurisdiction over cases concerning the *aides*, *tailles* and *gabelles* . . . irrespective of the importance, privileges and franchises of the persons involved, in both civil and criminal matters, will normally belong and appertain in the first instance to the *élus*, *grenetiers*, superintendants and other judges of the *aides*, each within his own boundaries and limits, whether *élections*, *greniers* or other jurisdictions, and in matters of appeal, to those who compose the sovereign court set up to deal with cases concerning the *aides*. In ordinary cases not involving the *aides*, competence belongs in the first instance to the bailiffs, *prévôts*, seneschals and other ordinary judges of the kingdom, and in matters of appeal, to our courts of *parlement* . . . be it known that we desire that the said royal directives, statutes and ordinances, drawn up, established and ordained by our predecessors concerning matters of jurisdiction, authority and cognizance arising out of the imposition of *aides*, *tailles* and *gabelles*, should be exactly kept, maintained and observed without infringement or derogation; and after having conveyed the above-mentioned ordinances, edicts, declarations, provisions, decrees and judgments to the members of our council and having received their opinions at a great gathering of princes of the blood and members of our council, held in our presence, bearing in mind the need to preserve the wellbeing of the state and the subsidies upon which our affairs depend, the need to protect and defend our kingdom, territories and *seigneuries* and the individuals, towns and areas within them, to resist and expel our enemies and adversaries; bearing in mind too other important considerations which have justly moved us, we have decided on the grounds both of our own knowledge and wishes and of the decision, judgment and conclusion of the above-mentioned counsellors, to confirm, commend, approve, ratify and sanction the said directives, ordinances, edicts, declarations, provisions, all the regulations contained in letters issued by our predecessors concerning matters of competence and jurisdiction arising out of the imposition of *aides, tailles* and *gabelles* so that henceforth neither our courts of *parlement* nor our ordinary judges and officers may cause any dispute, quarrel, disturbance or obstruction in these matters. . . .

59. FROM IBID., pp. 170 *et seq.*, June 1517, Ordinance concerning the *aides, tailles* and *gabelles*.

Francis, by the grace of God, king of France, to all those who will see these letters, greetings. For the defence, protection and safeguarding of our kingdom, territories, lands and *seigneuries* and in order to resist and hinder the enterprises of our enemies against the kingdom and Crown of France, our royal predecessors have seen fit to raise and maintain a large body of soldiers. In order to pay them and to bear the other great expenses, burdens and needs which the incidence of war has forced them to support and sustain, our predecessors have been compelled to augment and multiply the impositions, *aides, tailles* —formerly called *fouages*—and *gabelles*. According to the ordinances of our predecessors concerning the *aides* and *gabelles* all manner of men are liable, except those who are specifically exempted by the ordinances, and therefore they ought to bring in a great deal of revenue; however, it has been brought to our notice that some of our subjects, almost the majority, of various conditions, even the richest and most affluent, have violated these ordinances in attempting every day to gain exemption, to plunder and defraud us of the taxes and funds due to us from the said *aides* and *gabelles*, diminishing our revenue to such an extent that there is good reason—and we might be obliged hereafter—to increase the burden on our wretched people, especially by means of the *taille*, to our very great regret, sorrow and affliction, for with all our heart and might we desire to relieve them and preserve them from exactions and oppression. Similarly, deceit, duplicity and abuses may be daily observed in connection with the *tailles*, and with the administration of justice in regard to the *aides, tailles* and *gabelles,* the result of a variety of causes including the non-residence and incapacity of our officers, which has contributed to the public expenses of the kingdom, to a reduction in our funds and a delay in their payment which could grow more serious if we did not take suitable measures.

Be it known, therefore, that in view of the above-mentioned facts and because we desire to raise and facilitate the collection of the proper revenues due from our *aides, tailles* and *gabelles* so that we can more easily reduce the *tailles,* and to eliminate the duplicity and abuses which have been and still are practised in regard to the *taille,* all for the relief of the body politic, and with the advice and resolution of the members of our council and of those responsible for financial affairs, we have ordered, ordained and enacted and hereby order, ordain and enact by royal edict and decree, the following ordinances, items, points and articles:

1. First, in accordance with the ancient ordinances issued by our royal predecessors ... we decree and ordain that the *élus* and clerks appointed by us to deal with the *aides* and *tailles* in the *élections* of our kingdom will exercise their office personally, will live and make their permanent home in the capital town and principal seat of their *élection* within three months of the publication of these letters under pain of deprivation of office. ...

3. Item, neither our *élus,* attorneys and clerks concerned with the *aides* and *tailles* nor our *grenetiers* and superintendants may hold an ordinary judicial office. ...

4. Item, our *élus* are supposed to tour [*chevaucher*] their *élections* to discover what property the inhabitants possess, but it has come to our notice that they are making little effort to perform this duty ... as a result of which it happens daily that in drawing up their assessment and division of the *taille* they do not know from whom to levy it, oppressing those who should be relieved and relieving those who should be taxed, so that their assessments lack equality. For this reason we most expressly direct our *élus* in future to tour their *élections* every year and make diligent enquiries about the property, the losses and the untoward incidents which they may discover in the various parishes. ...

7. Item, although our *tailles* ought to be borne and paid by all manner of tax-payers, the strong assisting the weak, it has come to our notice nevertheless that the richest and most affluent are those who pay the least and who try to gain exemption whether by claiming to be nobles when they are manifestly not or by claiming to be tenants and *lessees* of churchmen or nobles, or in some other way, thus adding to the burden of our poor people. Therefore we hereby direct our *élus,* each in his own *élection,* to enquire in the course of

their visitations [*chevauchées*] whether all the inhabitants of the parishes of their *élections* are subject to the said *tailles* and where they discover anyone liable for the tax who has been left out of the assessment or who has not been justly assessed on their property, they will see that a just tax is imposed by the residents and tax-gathers of the parish concerned. . . .

8. Item, in so far as certain towns in our kingdom, certain places, colleges and communities and also certain individuals, including our officers as well as others, claim to be free and exempt from the payment of *tailles, aides* and *gabelles,* we ordain that all towns, places, colleges, communities, our officers and other individuals shall be subject to payment of the *tailles,* the strong supporting the weak, with the exception of those who by royal ordinance or by special immunity duly confirmed, verified and drawn up by us . . . are exempt and may enjoy their exemption fully and peaceably; and we direct our *élus* to compel those who claim privilege to show and demonstrate their immunity and in the case of those whose claims have not been duly and adequately verified and registered in the courts, to subject them to payment of the *tailles,* just like other non-privileged individuals. . . .

20. We forbid any of our officers or soldiers . . . to take part in tax-farming or to form any association or company with tax-farmers, and if they should do so, inadvertently or by error, it is our will that their share should be sold by auction. . . .

26. Item, in following the decrees and ordinances of our predecessors it is our will that the *grenetiers,* superintendents and measurers instituted by us in the *greniers* of our kingdom, shall exercise their offices personally without the assistance of lieutenants, and shall permanently reside in the town and place where the *grenier* of which they are the officers is situated. . . .

46. Item, in order to prevent the diminution and loss of funds due from *gabelles* caused by dealers in contraband salt who have sold and distributed untaxed salt within the limits and boundaries of our *greniers* and have avoided capture by banding themselves together in a large, armed group to defend themselves against our commissioners and officers, we hereby will and ordain that our generals of finance, each in the area under his command, will make enquiries about the places, ports and crossings where the said dealers make their way into the territory controlled by the *greniers,* whether from the direction of Brittany or Poitou, and will then inform us so that we may set up commissioners and guards at each of these places, ports, crossings and elsewhere . . . ; we command and charge the commissioners to ensure that the dealers in contraband salt do not enter the part of the country subject to

the *gabelle*; and if these dealers defend themselves in such a way that the commissioners and guards need aid and assistance, they will inform the noblemen of the area, our officers and others, all of whom we charge, under pain of disobedience, to give them help, advice, succour, assistance ... so that we may be obeyed and our authority maintained. ...

60. FROM D. J. BUISSERET, *Annales de Normandie*, XIII, 'Lettres Inédites de Sully aux Trésoriers Généraux de France à Caen 1599–1610)', No. 32, p. 293.

Sirs,

I am writing this letter so that you may see to it that the collector-general of finances in your office who was operating during the year 1607 makes haste to submit to the council his statement of accounts for that year, which he ought to have done already, having allowed the whole of the year 1608 and five months of the present year to slip by. Seeing that such slowness only brings confusion, if the collector-general still refuses to obey me on this matter, I beseech you to make him. You can either put his office in commission until he gives satisfaction, or, if he is not filling the office during this year, you can stop his salary through his associate in office, forbidding him to draw any until he has satisfied the council and given an account of his administration during the year in question. ...

... Fontainebleau, this fourth of June, 1609. ...

On the back: To the treasurers-general of France at the *bureau des finances* set up at Caen.

61 (a). FROM IBID., no. 29, pp. 290-1.

Sirs,

If my previous letters and the well-known causes of this year's expenses[1] were not sufficient explanation of the considerations which have prevented the king from reducing the level of taxation next year, I would perhaps take time to elaborate them further. But having already informed you of them when I sent you the warrant authorising the levy of the *taille (brevet de la taille)* and in the belief that nobody can still be unaware of them, I will take this opportunity to ask you to do your duty and to entreat you to do your utmost to see that the *tailles* and the extraordinary supplement for the year 1607, which allow his Majesty to offer little relief or reduction, will be uniformly raised. You know better than anybody the alleviation which the people would feel in their time of need if the king's taxes were imposed and levied

---

[1] The taking of Sedan, Spring, 1606.

K

according to the regulations issued by his council; you are also aware that no other officers have as much lawful cause nor as much power as you have to enforce their observance. I beseech you, therefore, to apply yourselves to that task and both by example and by your orders, compel the other officers to observe them exactly. A progress made by each of you through the *élections* of your department, undertaken with a little care and diligence can cure abuses which are of everyday occurrence there. Do not begrudge the small amount of time and trouble involved....

Fontainebleau, this sixteenth of November, 1606.

61 (b). FROM IBID., No. 30, pp. 291–2.

Sirs,

Some time ago I wrote asking you to send me an accurate and complete statement of the total value of the finances of your *généralité*, whether from the domain or from *gabelles*, other duties, subsidies, legal dues and dues of every other kind, and each and every tax over and above, whether on sales or alienations, fiefs and donations, rents, securities, in general everything which contributes to the said funds. A good two years ago a council decree was drawn up, which I sent to you, ordering that the treasurers of France should remain responsible in their own names for all omissions which might be discovered under the list of receipts in your statement of the total value of finances [in your *généralité*]. Yet despite this, I have been assured that you are not fulfilling your obligations, that you are leaving in the hands of general and particular collectors responsible for the domain, the *aides* and the *tailles*, certain funds which you can later dispose of as you wish. I am now reiterating this injunction in order that you may explain matters and send me so complete and accurate a statement, having regard to both receipts and expenses, that no cause for censure may remain, a statement in which you will specify all the funds that the collectors responsible for the domain, or other collectors, can have in their possession, referring not only to the present year but to past years as well. Confident that you will not fail me, I pray that the Creator may preserve you; from Paris, this fifteenth of August, 1607....

62 (a). FROM O. RANUM, *Richelieu and the Councillors of Louis XIII*, p. 157, Bullion and Bouthillier to Richelieu, February 1636.

The principal difficulty before us is whether we should make prisoners of all the *traitants*. The entire council of Finance and especially the Treasurer are protesting about the complete ruin of finances with regard to the *traitants*. If we put pressure on them, then most of them would go bankrupt; it would seem appropriate that your Eminence have a council held in his presence where you will take the trouble to hear them all, and afterwards your Eminence would make any decision which he pleased with His Majesty, which we will have executed immediately.

62 (b). FROM IBID., pp. 137–8, Richelieu to Séguier and Bouthillier, October 1641.

If Messieurs of the council continue to let the farmers and *traitants* unrestrainedly treat the king's subjects according to their own uncontrolled appetite, there will be some disorders in France similar to those in Spain. . . . In desiring too much we will reduce affairs to nothing and have nothing at all, and in banishing commerce we will deprive France of that on which she has mainly survived. I place on Messieurs of the council the responsibility for disorders which can happen by the malice of the *traitants* and others similar to them, and implore you to punish some of them so that the others will be constrained by their example.

62 (c). FROM IBID., pp. 175–6, Bouthillier to Richelieu, February 1642.

I am charged by the council to render account to his Eminence about what happened last Wednesday on the subject of the latest lease [to collect] the *aides* granted to the *Sire* de Forcoal, clerk in the *conseil des parties,* and the company joined with him; upon which a bid was made again at 100,000 *livres* for each year over and above what is stated in the last lease, for which even those who made the bid offered to deposit 300,000 *livres* in the treasury, or even up to 500,000 *livres,* so they said. This offer was placed in the hands of Monseigneur the Prince [Condé] (who comes to our *conseils de finances et direction* every day). We apologize, Monsieur the Chancellor and I, for having the bid brought into a full council session, and for hearing [in council] the *Sire* de Forcoal (who is called Saint-André and speaks for those who were making the bid with him). . . . Saint-André, who up to that moment had named few acceptable backers, proposed that the 300,000 *livres* or 500,000 *livres* which he had offered to deposit in the treasury, fall as a complete loss to him and his company if he did not give acceptable backers. He had previously proposed what were very good ones, including Rambouillet and Tallement [Talmond], but having sent to inquire two days before, they told us that they had never thought about it, and that they had a big enough task with the *cinq grosses fermes*. The council, therefore, on what was amply presented from both sides, having deliberated whether the bid should be accepted, rejected it unanimously—except for Monseigneur the Prince, Messieurs de Machault and de Mauroy, whom Saint-André and his company has assured at his house before the council, that I would be content with the backers which they had presented to me, which was not the case. It [the council] rejected the bid by twenty-eight votes to three. . . .

63 (a). FROM NOUVEAU RECUEIL DE REGISTRES DOMESTIQUES LIMOUSINS ET MARCHOIS, *Journal Domestique de Martial de Gay de Nexon, Lieutenant-Général à Limoges*, vol. I, pp. 457–8.

In the month of June [1591] the consuls raised a loan of twelve thousand crowns, the contract being witnessed by Monsieur Turquant,[1] and my contribution was assessed at one hundred crowns. The collectors of the said loan . . . came to ask for my assessment; I was told that if I did not pay, the dragoons would be sent to my home. I presented a petition asking that those responsible for sequestering my salary . . . should be compelled to pay my salary so that the debt owing on the loan might be met. Monsieur Turquant ordered that my petition should be served on the collector, the consuls and the royal attorney and the latter agreed that my salary should be paid.

63 (b). FROM *Extrait des Registres de l'Hôtel de Ville du Mans*, ed. T. Cauvin, Le Mans, 1835, p. 65.

1638.   All the notables of this town are obliged, by judgment of the general council, to sign a procuration to borrow the sum of 16,000 *livres*, in the hope that they may obtain discharge thereby from the obligation to provide the sum of 55,000 *livres* which His Majesty has asked for. Each notable who refuses to sign will be compelled personally to lend 600 *livres* in pursuance of the *intendant*'s decree. The *Sire* du Baril, a *bourgeois*, drew his sword against the usher who sought to induce him to lend 600 *livres* to the town. Proceedings were instituted against him on a charge of contumacy and the case was referred to the lieutenant-general with orders to lead the prosecution in the council. There followed an ordinance from Monsieur de la Ferté, the *intendant*, putting the *Sire* du Baril out of court; requiring the lieutenant-general in Paris to be notified of the decision not to pursue the charge of contumacy; and ordaining in addition that the notables, by signing the procuration in question, would be freed from any sort of coercion.

[1] *Intendant* at Limoges, he was sent in 1588 to revoke the powers of the Governor who favoured the Catholic League, as did Gay de Nexon.

63 (c). FROM IBID., p. 69.

1641. M. de Villayer, the *intendant* in the *généralité* of Tours, discharged some residents from their obligation to pay a *franc-fief* tax on the grounds that they had informed him that they no longer possessed land liable for this contribution: and in the case of those who did possess such land, he reduced their tax by a fifth. The municipal council resolved that, without suspending the ordinances of the *intendant*, the tax-roll would be adhered to; that it was not the *intendant* but the lieutenant-general who had been commissioned to act in this matter; that plaintiffs had to appear before the lieutenant-general and at his command would have to relinquish, for the benefit of the town, land for which they were liable to pay a tax of *franc-fief* if they were found to own such land, having previously denied the fact.

63 (d). FROM IBID., p. 81.

1646. The *intendant* is ordering the municipal council to raise immediately the sum of 30,000 *livres* from which the tax on the wealthy and 5,000 *livres* for expenses are to be deducted. Having received remonstrances upon the need to summon the general council of the town in order to hear its opinion, the *intendant* has issued a further ordinance convening it and has forbidden the tax-roll to be drawn up in the deputies' absence.

64. FROM B. PORCHNEV, *Les Soulèvements Populaires en France de 1623 à 1648*, French edn., Paris, 1963, p. 288.
Parlement of Rennes to Séguier, n.d.

Novelty always has a formidable and powerful capacity for causing apprehension among those who witness its introduction. This province has not been accustomed to hear the title of *intendant* of justice nor to witness the exercise of that office. The people are brought up to hear the king's wishes expressed through the agency of their ordinary magistrates, and subsequently to obey them as good and faithful subjects. The *parlement* makes its contribution by exericising the authority which the king has committed to it, acting towards the same end as he, namely to see that the king is faithfully served, his commands executed, justice honestly administered and the people sustained in peace. When justice is confided in a single person who frequently abuses his functions, great harm results which subsequently falls on the people who are made restless by new sufferings. If the king's finances in this province needed supervision, if justice was not properly maintained, if the people had given some indication that the magistrates were not prompt in issuing warrants, then recourse could be had to these extraordinary remedies. But we thank God that there is no need for any adjustment. This *parlement,* which can judge the consequences more readily than those who are at a distance and can see to the prevention of all complaints and disturbances, believes that the king and you, Monseigneur, should approve of its opposition to this office of *intendant,* which only reproduces the function of ordinary judges whilst unsettling them in their offices and which could lead to ... an increased burden for the people in the shape of new costs and the consequent framing of complaints by the people against this novelty.

65 (a). FROM J. F. BLUCHE, *L'Origine des Magistrats du Parlement de Paris,* Paris, 1956, The Bochart de Saron Family.

IV   Jean IV Bochart, *seigneur* of Champigny, councillor in the *parlement* [of Paris] (1563), *maître des requêtes* (1567)....

V   Jean V. B. (died 1630), *seigneur* of Novay and Champigny, *maître des requêtes* (1585), president in the chamber of *enquêtes* in the *parlement* [of Paris] (1594), councillor of state, *intendant* at Poitiers, ambassador in Venice, controller-general then superintendant of finance, first president of the *parlement* [of Paris] (1628), died in office....

VI   François B. of Champigny (died 1665), *seigneur* of Saron, councillor in the *Grand Conseil, maître des requêtes,* councillor of state, *intendant* in Provence (1637), at Grenoble and at Lyons....

65 (b). FROM IBID., The Lefèvre de Caumartin de Boissy Family.

II   Jean Ier Lefèvre (died before 1560), esquire, *seigneur* of Caumartin and Villers, treasurer of France in Picardy (1555), died in office....

III Jean II L. (died in Paris 1579), esquire, *seigneur* of Caumartin and St-Port, treasurer of France (1564)....

IV   Louis Ier L. (1552–1623), *seigneur* of Caumartin and Boissy, baron of St-Port, councillor in the *parlement* [of Paris] (1579), *maître des requêtes* (1585), *intendant* of Amiens (1590), councillor of state (1594), ambassador in Spain (1605), keeper of the seals (1622); he married in 1582 Marie Miron, daughter of Robert, *intendant* of finance.

V   Louis II L. (died 1624), *seigneur* of the same estates, councillor in the *Grand Conseil, maître des requêtes,* president in the chamber of *requêtes* [of the *parlement* of Paris], *intendant* of Picardy and councillor of state, died whilst undertaking an embassy to Venice. He married Madeleine de Choisy in 1622, daughter of Jean, *seigneur* of Balleroy, private secretary to the king and collector-general at Caen.

66. FROM IBID., The Bèze Family.

I.   Jean Ier de Bèze, *bourgeois* of Vézelay.
II   Jean II de B. (died before 1604), merchant at Taunay. . . .
III Claude Ier de B. (Taunay 1585–*ibid* 1650), *seigneur* of Lys, *élu* at Clamecy, secretary to Marguerite of Valois. . . .
IV   Claude II de B. (born 1625), *seigneur* of Lys, Pignol, Talon, etc., *élu* at Clamecy. . . .
V   Jacques de B. (born 1655), esquire, *seigneur* of Lys, ennobled by the office of private secretary to the king. . . .

67 (a). FROM B. PORCHNEV, *Les Soulèvements Populaires en France de 1623 à 1648*, pp. 185–6.
Letter of the *duc* d'Epernan [governor of Guyenne] to Séguier, n.d.

I learned at Grenade in a letter from the aldermen [*jurats*] of Bordeaux that a revolt was feared there as a result of the rumour of a new imposition of the *sou* per *livre* tax, and upon receiving this news I set out at once for Bordeaux. Yesterday in letters sent by the same aldermen and by the first president [of the *parlement* of Bordeaux] I learned that Monsieur de Lanson (the *intendant*) whom the people suspected of being at Bordeaux to supervise this imposition, had left the town on the advice of the *parlement* and had been accompanied by the aldermen, as he himself wished, as far as the boat that was to take him to Bourg. . . With God's help I shall reach Bordeaux in two days and do all that I can to maintain order and stifle a sedition which could flare up and spread very easily in this province because of the extraordinary expense of supporting soldiers which it has borne for five months and is still sustaining, the difficulty of paying *tailles* and other royal revenues, the discontent of the office-holders in the *parlement* and in the *présidial* courts because of the half-yearly arrangements [*semestres*],[1] the separation of jurisdictions and the establishment of new tribunals with which they are threatened.

67 (b). FROM IBID., pp. 250–1.
Letter of Marshal Schomberg [governor of Languedoc] to Séguier, July 4, 1645.

You will have learned from the accounts sent to you by Messieurs

---

[1] The number of judges was doubled, each group serving in turn.

de Bosquet and de Balthazar [*intendants*] as well as from the official report of the chief judge of this town [Montpellier] of the sedition which broke out in June. It only lasted for three days, but during this short time houses and household goods were set on fire and murder and other crimes committed. . . . I have now armed all the judicial and financial bodies in the town, and those excellent merchants who had not taken up arms came to ask my pardon for the remainder and promised to arm themselves, which they did, and for two days peace has reigned in the town because of the orders which I gave to prevent the levying of taxes for the *joyeux avènement*[1] which caused the uprising. Truly, Monsieur, these taxes are excessive and since they include all the craft-masters the disorders have been started by the craftsmen's wives and then taken up by the husbands. There were no *bourgeois* nor worthy merchants involved in the affair but the tax-farmers are so detested in this town that nobody went to very much trouble to prevent the disturbance. Everybody in the town thanks God that I am here; it would indeed have been a dreadful situation if I had not come and one half of the town had slaughtered the other half. I am awaiting the Queen's orders on this matter; the council will judge its importance better than anybody.

68. FROM IBID., pp. 115–6.

Letter from Lozières, (*intendant* of Dauphiné) to Séguier, October 5, 1644.

Royal needs have forced us to offer something which in less pressing times we would doubtless have taken care not to do. We have taken into account the fact that the majority of communities in this province have not yet shown any readiness to raise the sums stipulated in the warrants which have been despatched to them, and we have recognized that the only way to persuade them to contribute a part of their payments was to give them some time before paying the remainder in which their deputies could demonstrate their want and obtain from the king the alleviation which they sought. If the total amount had been demanded in one payment, then undoubtedly little or nothing would have been obtained, considering the attitude of the majority of people in this province which was to start a general revolt rather than pay the whole sum. It is true that in many areas their poverty is so great that even if they had been willing, they would have been quite unable to meet the demands made of them. . . . The snowfalls which, it is being said, exceed those of any previous year, have rotted almost all the grain. . . . The frosts which have come late and have

---

[1] Tax levied at the accession of each new king in confirmation of rights and privileges previously held.

affected the country around Paris, have also damaged the pasture lands and vineyards in this part of the world, so that this province could scarcely be in a less capable position to pay large sums than it is at present. I declare that if you do not grant great relief and if you ordain that they will still be required to pay a considerable amount more than they are now expected to pay, it will be very difficult to enforce obedience and the risk of some new disorders will be great since in most parts of this country the people simply cannot pay. . . . Monseigneur de Lesdiguières [*duc* de L., governor of Vienne] and I have not granted a reprieve on payments due in past years for if we had done that not only would the subsequent levy have been much more difficult to collect but we would also have been rewarding in some measure the default of those who were able to pay but had not done so.

69. FROM IBID., Appendix 31.
Letter from Bosquet, royal *intendant* in Languedoc, to Séguier.

Monseigneur, two matters have occurred in the province which I must report to you so that you may be in a position to give whatever orders are necessary.

First, Monseigneur, a decree has been issued by the *parlement* of Toulouse, a copy of which I am attaching to this letter. Mischief makers have made this a pretext to stir up the people in various places and to persuade them to refuse payment of taxes, chiefly in upper Languedoc whence those who have the task of collecting taxes by virtue of extraordinary warrants now suspended by this decree, have withdrawn, bringing their complaints to me and asking me to ensure the safeguarding and protection of their persons. It has even been reported to me that a tax-gatherer [*collecteur*] has been killed in Toulouse by the enraged people and the same thing has very nearly happened at Lavaur. Current rumours have made of the decree far more than its actual terms justify and the people cannot be disabused of the idea that according to this decree they are only obliged to pay the ancient royal *taille*, that all extraordinary commissions, including those of the *intendants*, have been revoked and that henceforth they will only be bound by orders emanating from the *parlement*. I am trying to dispel all these false rumours and up to this moment I do not believe that any great harm has been done but what may follow is to be feared to this extent that I understand that under the pretext of preserving public well-being, the bishops in some dioceses, where they have absolute control, are not doing all that they could to persuade the people of where their duty lies. I gave this as my opinion shortly after the Cardinal's death [Richelieu] forseeing then at an exclusively clerical assembly held in the diocese of Narbonne, that individuals were not so disposed to render obedience as they had been in the past. I took action, issued a writ and had the matter taken before the council. I have written about it to M. d'Hemery in order to have a decree issued confirming my orders; that procedure was approved yet I am still awaiting the decree three to four months later. I have seen sedition beginning to break out in Guyenne and although I am aware of the difference in the people's attitude and of the difference in governorship in this province and know likewise that at the moment there is no need to fear a similar situation here, nevertheless there is no doubt that if the two sovereign companies of this province are not kept in order and if the prelates are not exhorted to see that the orders of the [king's] council are executed, in a short time the people will be in revolt, not from any spontaneous movement, because they are incapable of that in this province, but as a result of the bad example which they will have received. . . .

Montpellier, June 22, 1643.   [signed]   Bosquet.

70. FROM R. MOUSNIER, J. P. LABATUT, Y. DURAND, *Deux Cahiers de la Noblesse*, p. 140.
    Cahier of the Remonstrances of the Nobility in the bailiwick of Troyes, 1651, Art. 23.

Now to come to the matter of the reformation of justice in your kingdom, Your Majesty is entreated to listen to the general complaints of the whole of France, concerning venality and the excessive price of judicial and financial offices, which is the cause of the widespread corruption discernible in those who exercise them. . . . The cause of this immensely high cost of offices may be traced to that enemy of the state, the *paulette*, palotte [sic] now called the annual due which in the manner of a canker is gradually undermining and consuming all the families of this kingdom, and therefore the nobility begs His Majesty most humbly to revoke the wretched annual due immediately and forever, with orders forbidding its re-establishment under any pretext whatsoever.

And may this be done on the last day of next December since the officers have not paid any loans nor made any advance payments since it has been continued and re-established this last time and all the nobility of the kingdom are entreated to unite in order to secure this present article, for it has an interest in seeing the prices of offices reduced and restored if possible to what they were in our fathers' time fifty or sixty years ago when a nobleman of the *robe* could call three or four of his children into public offices; now only tax-farmers can do that and it is even impossible for a nobleman who follows the profession of arms to place any of his children (although they are capable) into offices of the *robe* because of their excessive and enormous price, and truly it is monstrous to witness this great superfluity and cost of office, not previously heard of nor even contemplated and unlikely to be believed by posterity.

We are therefore now obliged most humbly to entreat Your Majesty to re-establish the ancient order, which obtained before the time of Louis XII; under that régime when a judicial office became vacant whether in the sovereign courts, on the royal benches or in subordinate jurisdictions, the officers in the place concerned elected three suitable persons capable of exercising the vacant office and the king conferred it upon one of the three, who did not have to spend a single *denier*; and because such offices had cost nothing their holders rendered justice freely and without fees (*épices*), content with the honour of being judges. Moreover, His Majesty's conscience was clear before God and his people.

71. FROM B. PORCHNEV, *Les Soulèvements Populaires en France de 1623 à 1648*, p. 96.
Letter from the *seigneur* of Montbrun to Séguier, April 1643.

Monseigneur, silence is blameworthy when there is a need for speech and attached as I am to the king's service and to the observance of your orders, I cannot pass over in silence what is happening in the area of Rouergue, very close to where I live; the example given there is being generally heeded by all the people in the surrounding districts, for their great wretchedness which passes belief tempts them to take very wrong resolutions which could only lead them to complete ruin. Monseigneur, I presume you have heard what happened eight days ago in Villefranche to Monsieur de la Ferrière, the *intendant* of justice in this province of Guyenne, from whom a turbulent band of two or three thousand people extorted by means of armed entreaties and remonstrances a number of regulations in their favour.... Monseigneur, since then this band or collection of soldiery and armed individuals has greatly increased in size inasmuch as it is certain that from every part of this bailiwick (which covers a wide area) people have been flocking in very large numbers and with weapons to Villefranche, in order to support and endorse the disturbances which have broken out. They are protesting, Monseigneur, that because of their extreme poverty they want to pay to the tax-farmers precisely what they owe the king, and nothing more than that....

DOCUMENT SOURCES

AUBERT, F., *Histoire du Parlement de Paris de l'Origine à François Ier*, 2 vols., Paris, 1894.

BEAUREPAIRE, C. de R. de (ed.), *Cahiers des Etats de Normandie, 1633-66*, Rouen, 1878.

BELLEGUISE, A., *Traité de la Noblesse et de son Origine, suivant les Préjugés rendus par les Commissaires députés pour la Vérification des Titres de Noblesse*, Paris, 1700.

BLOCH, M., *Les Rois Thaumaturges*, Paris, 1924.

BLUCHE, J. F., *L'Origine des Magistrats du Parlement de Paris*, Paris, 1956.

BODIN, J., *The Six Bookes of a Commonweale*, ed. K. D. McRae, Cambridge, Mass., 1962.

BRANTÔME, Pierre de Bourdeille, seigneur de, *Oeuvres Complètes*, ed. L. Lalanne, Paris, 1867.

BUISSERET, D. J., 'Lettres Inédites de Sully aux Trésoriers Généraux de France à Caen (1599-1610)', *Annales de Normandie*, XIII, 1963.

CAUVIN, T. (ed.), *Extrait des Registres de l'Hôtel de Ville du Mans*, Le Mans, 1835.

CHÉRIN, L., *Abrégé Chronologique d'Edits, Déclarations, Règlements, Arrêts et Lettres Patentes des Rois de France de la Troisième Race, concernant le Fait de Noblesse*, Paris, 1788.

DOOLIN, P. R., *The Fronde*, Harvard, 1935.

DUMONT, J. (ed.), *Corps Universel Diplomatique du Droit des Gens*, 8 vols. Amsterdam, 1726-39.

FONTANON, A. (ed.), *Les Edits et Ordonnances des Rois de France*, 3 vols., Paris, 1611.

FOURQUEVAUX, Raymond de Beccarie de Pavie, sieur de, *Instructions sur le Faict de la Guerre*, ed. G. Dickinson, London, 1954.

FRANÇOIS, M. (ed.), *Lettres de Henri III, Roi de France*, 2 vols., Paris, 1965.

GARNIER, J. (ed.), *Chartes de Communes et d'Affranchissements en Bourgogne*, 3 vols., Dijon, 1877.

GARNIER, J. (ed.), *Correspondance de la Mairie de Dijon*, 3 vols., Dijon, 1868-70.

GODEFROY, T. and D., *Le Cérémonial Français*, 2 vols., Paris, 1649.

GUIBERT, L. (ed.), *Nouveau Recueil de Registres Domestiques Limousins et Marchois*, 2 vols., Limoges, 1895-1903.

HAILLAN, Bernard de Girard, seigneur du, *De l'Etat et Succès des Affaires de France*, Paris, 1609.

HÔPITAL, Michel de l', *Oeuvres Inédites*, ed. J. Dufey, 2 vols., Paris, 1825.

ISAMBERT, F.-A. (ed.), *Recueil Général des Anciennes Lois Françaises*, 29 vols., Paris, 1822-33.

JACQUETON, G. (ed.), *Documents relatifs à l'Administration Financière en France de Charles VII à François Ier (1443-1523)*, Paris, 1891.

LA LANDE DE CALAN, C. de (ed.), *Documents Inédits relatifs aux Etats de Bretagne de 1491 à 1589*, 2 vols., Rennes, 1908-9.

LA ROQUE, G. de, *Traité de la Noblesse*, new ed., Rouen, 1735.

LA ROQUE, G. de, *Traité du Ban et Arrière-Ban*, Paris, 1676.

LOYSEAU, C., *Traité des Ordres*, Paris, 1613.

LOYSEAU, C., *Cinq Livres du Droit des Offices avec le Livre des Seigneuries et celui des Ordres*, Paris, 1614.

LUCINGE, René de, sire de Les Allymes, *Dialogue du François et du Savoysien (1593)*, ed. A. Dufour, Paris, 1963.

MASSELIN, J., *Journal des Etats-Généraux de France tenus à Tours en 1484*, ed. A. Bernier, Paris, 1835.

MAUGIS, E., *Histoire du Parlement de Paris de l'Avènement des Rois Valois à la Mort d'Henri IV*, 3 vols., Paris, 1913-16.

MAYER, C. J., *Des Etats-Généraux et autres Assemblées Nationales*, 18 vols., Paris, 1788-9.

MOUSNIER, R., LABATUT, J. P., DURAND, Y. (eds.), *Deux Cahiers de la Noblesse*, Paris, 1965.

Ordonnances des Rois de France. Règne de François Ier, 7 vols., Paris, 1902-41.
Ordonnances des Rois de France de la Troisième Race, 22 vols., Paris, 1723-1849.

PASQUIER, E., *Les Recherches de la France*, Paris, 1596.

PITHOU, P., *Les Libertés de l'Eglise Gallicane*, 5 vols., Lyons, 1771.

PORCHNEV, B., *Les Soulèvements Populaires en France de 1623 à 1648*, French ed., Paris, 1963.

RADOUANT, R. (ed.), *Actions et Traités Oratoires de Guillaume du Vair*, Paris, 1911.

RANUM, O., *Richelieu and the Councillors of Louis XIII*, Oxford, 1963.

Recueil des Actes, Titres et Mémoires concernant les Affaires du Clergé de France, 13 vols., Paris, 1716-64.

SAINT-SIMON, Louis de Rouvroy, duc de, *Mémoires*, ed. A. de Boislisle, 41 vols., Paris, 1879-1928.

SEYSSEL, Claude de, *La Monarchie de France*, ed. J. Poujol, Paris, 1961.

SPANHEIM, E., *Relation de la Cour de France en 1690*, ed. E. Bourgeois, Paris, 1900.

TALON, O., *Mémoires continués par Denis Talon*, vol. XXX of *Nouvelle Collection des Mémoires relatifs à l'Histoire de France depuis le XIIIe siècle jusqu' à la fin du XVIIIe siècle*, ed. J. F. Michaud and J. J. F. Poujoulat, 34 vols., Paris, 1854.

VALENTIN-SMITH and GUIGUE, C. (eds.), *Bibliotheca Dumbensis, ou Recueil de Chartes, Titres et Documents pour servir à l'Histoire de Dombes*, 2 vols., Trévoux, 1854-85.

VOLTAIRE, F. M. Arouet de, *Catéchisme du Curé* in *Dictionnaire Philosophique*, Geneva, 1764.

INDEX